persons, but he found both hope and healing with a level of determination and conviction that is unmatched. *The Unbound Man* is a courageous story of traumatic lifetime experiences, but it also describes an approach and roadmap to both hope and healing for men where they can find renewed purpose and meaning in their lives.

*Denny Stoecklin*
*Chairman of Helping Men Heal/The Well*
*Retired CFO of Concordia University- Portland*

Matt is tackling a subject that's "left behind" in culture, one that impacts generations, culture and community. Tere's hope and, while based in trauma, the stories of redemption provide us the courage to press forward; *The Unbound Man* is the guidebook.

*Jef Rogers*
*Chairman of OneAccord*

An extremely powerful story of a young man, from his childhood days through his young adulthood years, who has experienced trauma. His eventual and unwavering faith prepared him for a life of humility before men, but through injustices – large and small – he came to realize that he would not remain a victim. Matt has chosen to tackle a subject that's "taboo" in our culture but historically impacts generations. Matt's story of *The Unbound Man* certainly, through examples of courage, provides the reader the opportunity to overcome and move forward.

*B. Maurice Ward, CDP, CV, MRT*
*Administrator/DSHS-(JJ&RA)*
*Director of Diversity & Inclusion*

Matt's story of his life journey is gripping and inspiring. He has a distinctive way of dealing with the complex subject of personal trauma in very understandable ways. The book is worth reading for practical insights alone, such as Healing Trauma Reminders and Insights for Loved Ones. Of particular delight to me were his insightful comments on our broken culture from his distinct, both Caucasian and African-American viewpoint. As a fighter pilot who survived the chaos and trauma of the Vietnam War, I could only say, "Matt, I would fly on your wing any day!"

*Dr. Ted Roberts*
*Bestselling Author, Pastor, Sexual Addiction and Trauma Counselor*

As Assistant Executive Director of an organization that represents state and local directors of the juvenile justice systems throughout the country, I believe that that Matt's book *The Unbound Man* provides an interesting, introspective look into how males view and respond to trauma in different ways, which left unaddressed often leads to destructive behaviors that can have long lasting impact on their lives. This is a must-read for not only males who are experiencing or have experienced trauma, but for anyone who lives, coaches or works with males of any age.

*Wendi Faulkner*
*Asst. Exec. Dir., Council of Juvenile Correctional Administrators*

Sexual, physical and emotional trauma are not topics we associate with men. Matt Burton has made it his mission to change that. Through this book Matt speaks with compassion and practiced encouragement to men who suffer from the effects of trauma. His personal accounts of several types of trauma and his journey toward healing are told frankly, and his determination and many uses of supportive groups and individuals lay a groundwork for

## PRAISE FOR THE UNBOUND MAN

This book is a must-read for men who have experienced trauma and know it, men who have experienced trauma and have been ignoring it, those who know men who have experienced trauma, and for professionals who help men deal with trauma. Matt's story is about hope and finding purpose and meaning that could set us free.

*Fariborz Pakseresht*
*Director, Oregon Department of Human Services*

*The Unbound Man* provides the breakthrough answer to the problems millions of men who struggle with trauma face today.

The world encourages broken traumatized men to "Man up:" to bury their brokenness and not confront or deal with the root causes of their issues. Questions like: "How did I end up this way?" and "How can I break the shackles of the traumatic experiences in my past and heal myself?" are answered in *The Unbound Man.*

The stories are *real,* and the solutions *heal.* The author tells his story in raw, authentic, and direct manner which will encourage traumatized men to come out from hiding and get on the path to recovery.

*The Unbound Man* is truly a breakthrough work that will heal millions. I highly recommend it!

*David Cole*
*Retired CEO of Outerwall (Coinstar/Redbox)*

Matt Burton opens the door to his soul with his book *The Unbound Man*. It is this opening that will provide a foundation for other men to share their stories, use his framework, and find their path to healing. Matt shows other men how their stories matter and courageously demonstrates through his words that they do not have to suffer in silence or go it alone. This book will become a staple of my professional library. It will be a tool and resource for those who are working on their journey of healing. *The Unbound Man* is a must-read for understanding the traumas men often face. This book is honest, raw and moving, but most of all – offers hope that healing is not only possible but achievable.

*Courtland McPherson, MSW, LCSW*
*Psychotherapist, CVO, Little Red Telescope Psychotherapy*

Matt Burton unflinchingly and honestly shares his experiences of trauma. He relays his stories knowing they will lift the burden of trauma of other men and let them know they aren't alone. *The Unbound Man* conveys a message of hope, healing, and solidarity.

*Anonymous*
*mother of a young man that took his own life*

LOVED IT! I already told my Special Treatment teams about it. Can't wait for them to read it. I think this will be EXTREMELY helpful to our youth.

Jennifer Jaworski, Psy.D., LCPC
Chief Of Mental Health, Illinois Department of Juvenile Justice

In our world today there are many trauma victims that are in desperate need of hope and don't know where to turn. Their life has lost direction and purpose. Matt Burton was one of those others to pursue their own healing. Every man should read this book.

*Philip W. Harris Ph.D.*
*Department of Criminal Justice, Temple University*

Trauma often leads to destructive behaviors, which can land men and kids in prison or the juvenile justice system. Matt is working to help men and youth recognize how their trauma is impacting their lives and behaviors and then helps guide them through the recovery journey.

Matt's book is timely for those of us within the criminal and juvenile justice systems who are beginning to tackle the issues of trauma affecting the men and youth we serve.

Understanding the traumas youth and adult prisoners have suffered can provide staff with an understanding of where certain behavioral issues come from, help them better recognize what triggers these behaviors, and provide them with insight that helps de-escalate situations and behaviors in way that improves the overall atmosphere and reduces incidents of violence within the "prison" setting. This book should be required reading for all staff working in correctional environments, particularly within the juvenile justice system."

*Mike Dempsey*
*Exec. Dir. Council of Juvenile Correctional Administrators (CJCA)*
*CJCA represents the youth correctional CEOs in 50 states, Puerto Rico, & major metropolitan counties*

Matt has written a guide—a call to heal—that is compassionate, non-judgmental and eminently approachable. But do not mistake accessibility for an uninformed perspective! It is very clear that Matt has experience and education behind his wisdom. However, he has chosen to bring a voice that welcomes, encourages, that never gives up hope over academic facts or promoting a particular curriculum. This is what many men—or those in their lives seeing them suffer—need most. This is done in the framework of his own immensely powerful story. Never boastful, never self-promoting, but instead selfless and positive. If you or a loved one even suspects they may have unresolved trauma, Matt has laid it all on the line for you. As someone who has seen some of the worst that trauma can do on a daily basis; as Matt's cancer surgeon I am someone who has seen Matt's fight, his positivity and his grace, I can truly say that this is an incredible book.

*S. David Cho, MD, FACS*
*Portland, Oregon*

All too often, we in corrections and the public focus solely on the trauma these men commit on others, not recognizing that they are in many cases reacting out of their own trauma.

Matt Burton's book, *The Unbound Man*, goes beyond the destructive behaviors that are the results of trauma from men. He peels back the pain and helps to shed light both through his own experiences and the experiences of others on the impact of unattended male trauma – not just to that man himself, but to others around him. Even better, he shares what worked for him to move beyond the trauma to find health and wholeness, to break the shackles of trauma. This book is a must read not just for justice Involved men, but also for those who work with them.

*Scott Semple*
*Retired Commissioner, Connecticut Department of Corrections*

Matthew Burton is a gift. He connects with people in a way that cannot be taught, and actively and consistently (and necessarily bluntly) reminds us that recovery is possible for those that commit to action. Matt has remarkable insight and compassion for survivors as well as those whose lives are impacted by the shockwave that emanates from personal trauma.

*Todd Marker*
*Partner, Alpine Pacific Capital, LLC*

Matt Burton courageously shares his story of discrimination, abuse, heartbreak, and trauma in a number of ways that men can relate to. In his story, you will find one common theme: the desire to help men heal. Regardless of your story or your current or past situation, Matt wants you to know you're not alone as he and other men walk beside you and as you find the strength to unbind yourself from shame.

*Sam Louie, M.A., LMHC*
*Psychotherapist, Speaker, Author of Asian Shame and Addiction:*
*Suffering in Silence*

Matt Burton thoughtfully confronts the messages that prevent men from understanding their trauma. He shows deep insight into how healing can happen, using examples from his own life to show that betterment really is possible.

*Chris Keefer*
*Foundation Trustee and Business Leader*

# THE UNBOUND MAN FOR CHRISTIANS

## BREAKING THE SHACKLES OF TRAUMA AND ABUSE EXPERIENCED BY MEN

### MATT BURTON

# THE UNBOUND MAN FOR CHRISTIANS

## BREAKING THE SHACKLES OF TRAUMA AND ABUSE EXPERIENCED BY MEN

Copyright © 2024 By Becoming Well, LLC

All rights reserved. No part of this book may be reproduced or transmitted in any form or by any means, electronic or mechanical, including photocopying, recording, or by information storage and retrieval system, without permission in writing from the copyright owner.

The views and opinions expressed in this book are those of the author and do not necessarily reflect the official policy or position of Becoming Well, LLC.

Published by Becoming Well, LLC.

www.MyBecomingWell.com

Library of Congress Control Number:
Paperback ISBN: 979-8-3302-9355-1
eBook ISBN: 979-8-3302-9357-5

Cover design by Debbie Lewis

*Printed in the United States of America*

## Table of Contents

ACKNOWLEDGMENTS ........................................................... XV

AUTHOR'S NOTE ................................................................. XIX

INTRODUCTION ................................................................... XXI

**PART ONE: MEN DO EXPERIENCE TRAUMA**

   1: WHY IT'S SO HARD FOR MEN TO DEAL WITH TRAUMA ........................................................................... 3

   2: MEN EXPERIENCE SEXUAL TRAUMA— FROM OTHER MALES ................................................................. 25

   3: MEN EXPERIENCE SEXUAL TRAUMA— FROM FEMALES TOO ................................................................... 41

   4: MEN EXPERIENCE PHYSICAL TRAUMA ..................... 57

   5: MEN EXPERIENCE EMOTIONAL TRAUMA ................ 71

   6: MEN EXPERIENCE LOSS, REJECTION AND ABANDONMENT ................................................................. 87

   7: MEN EXPERIENCE MEDICAL TRAUMA ..................... 109

**PART TWO: MEN CAN HEAL FROM TRAUMA**

   8: THE DOOR TO HEALING OPENS .................................. 129

   9: BREAKING FREE FROM THE SHACKLES BY "GOING THERE" ................................................................. 145

   10: BREAKING FREE FROM THE SHACKLES ................ 165

   11: BREAKING FREE FROM THE SHACKLES ................ 187

   12: BREAKING FREE FROM THE SHACKLES ................ 205

   13: WHEN MEN HEAL FROM TRAUMA, EVERYBODY WINS ..................................................................................... 223

TOOLS THAT HELPED ME ................................................................. 235
SOURCES FOR STATISTICS ......................................................... 239
BIBLIOGRAPHY/SUGGESTED READING ............................... 241
ABOUT THE AUTHOR ................................................................... 245

# ACKNOWLEDGMENTS

Behind this book stands an almost countless number of people who helped, encouraged and ultimately believed in me or my story and, more importantly, believed that men and boys have not only been the deliverers of trauma but also the recipients of trauma. That. That we deserve and have permission to pursue healing. That. That we don't have to remain bound to our pain. That. That we can break the shackles that trauma has bound us to, and that our healing will help those we love, those that our trauma has impacted, to have the opportunity to find healing as well.

Tanks to all those who have helped me on my spiritual journey over the past almost thirty years, especially Ted Roberts, Jim Andrew, Rita Nussli and the folks at East Hill Church and Cascade Presbyterian Church.

Thanks to the many counselors and clinicians that have helped to advance my own healing since 1992. I need to say a special thanks to Greg Hasek, who guided me to another level in breaking out of the prison of trauma that I thought I would be trapped in for the rest of my life. And I can't ever thank Dr. Howard Fradkin and Jim Struve enough for helping me, along with our staff, to lead the training of more than 1,500 mental health clinicians on male trauma. Andre Pruitt, who also helped with the training, additionally taught me that regardless of what I've heard in the past, I am Black enough already regardless of what some unaccepting folks in the black community may say.

Thanks to all those who attended the thousands of 12-Step meetings with me over the past twenty-seven years, with a special shout-out to Erich, Lud, Mike, Christine and my other sponsors along the way.

Thanks to my coaches Kathie England (my ADD coach) and Kirsten Hawes (my executive/life coach). You've helped me organize, prioritize and execute my life.

Thanks to John Castles, Fariborz Pakseresht, Chuck Weir, Lynn and Maria Sheehan, as well as Mike and Donna Hill for your unwavering encouragement and belief in me and in this work.

Thanks to Jon Hartinger D.O. and Providence for recognizing there might be something wrong and having me tested, as well as Dr. Sungeyun David Cho and all the great people at Kaiser who cared for me through all the ups and downs that my cancer brought on.

Tanks to Scott Klusmann, Denny Stoecklin, Dave Cole, Concordia University-Portland and to all those that invested time and money in the non-profit and social purpose for-profit organizations I've led over the years, all with the heart and focus of advancing healing to those that were hurting. Like me, you invested not just for financial reasons, but to see men's lives change. Though many of us lost our financial investments through some of these endeavors, your investment impacted countless men's lives and is still paying them and our community dividends.

Tanks to Wendi Faulkner, Digene Farrar, Courtland McPherson, Sam Louie, Chris Montovino, Chris and Christine Keefer, Karen Maseng, and the others already mentioned above that reviewed and provided feedback on the book. To Kevin, for your input and guidance throughout this writing process. To Lindsey Keefer for editing and Michael Klassen and your team at Illumify on the publishing side. Thanks as well to Todd Marker, the Keefer Family, and the late Ken Austin, all of whose early sponsorship investments gave us the financial wherewithal to see this to completion.

To my sons Jeremiah and Jaden and daughter Cali Burton Talbot, I love you all very much and hope that as I continue to heal, the impact of my unattended past trauma on you may be healed, and that my continued healing will benefit you. And thank you to my mom and dad, Roy and Mary Burton, who built into me a stubbornness and ability to persevere.

The person I want to and need to thank the most is the one all this has cost the most. The cost of my healing process has been high and has impacted no one more than my wife Laura. She is the unsung hero of this work, and I, as well as men everywhere, say thank you for not giving up on me and not giving up on this work of helping men heal.

Finally, and sincerely, I want to thank God, not just figuratively, but literally. Originally, through all my trials, I believed he had abandoned me. But I learned through my healing journey that he actually was the one that carried me through.

## AUTHOR'S NOTE

The stories from my life that are included in this book are true and accurate, as best as I can recall them from my memory and my experience. Stories that are drawn from the experience of other people represent my best attempt to chronicle events and situations that were shared with me by those involved. I apologize for any inadvertent errors or inaccuracies. Some names and identifying details in the personal stories in this book have been changed to protect the privacy of individuals.

This book is not a substitution for consultation with healthcare professionals. As the author, I urge readers to consult with licensed healthcare professionals.

*Matt Burton*

*www.TheUnboundMan.com*

## INTRODUCTION

The book you are about to read is a book I never would have expected to write. Back in high school, the only reading material my English teacher ever found me studying was the latest issue of *Sports Illustrated*. The only way I was ever going to write a book would be after I became a pro basketball star and I got to tell everybody exactly how I achieved my dream.

But things change. Life tosses obstacles in our path and we have to figure out how to sidestep or hurdle them. We find ourselves going in new and unexpected directions. Sometimes we feel like we're dangling off the edge of a cliff. Today, at the age of fifty-two, if you put me in a room with a group of men meeting for the first time and asked us to name our greatest achievement in life, my answer would make other guys look at me a little weird:

> ***My greatest accomplishment is making the choice to address the major trauma and loss in my life, to begin a healing journey, and to follow it wherever it takes me, for as long as it takes.***

That's it. I've spent the last twenty-eight years of my life healing from the first twenty-four years. This accomplishment comes with no big title, no claim to fame or fortune, no list of awards. That doesn't matter to me. Healing from trauma has been the most fulfilling journey of my life. It has enabled me to live a life of meaning and purpose, with a loving and healthy marriage, two extraordinary teenage sons and an amazing adult daughter who has blessed us with three grandchildren.

There's something else my one major accomplishment has done for me. It opened the door to a new mission. Today, I am able to serve as an evangelist—a conduit, guide or messenger helping other men suffering from all kinds of trauma and loss to break the shackles of hurt and pain and seek health and wholeness in their lives. This book is born from that mission. It's my way of giving back after so much has been given to me.

I'm here to assure you that no matter what trauma you suffered, and no matter how much your life has been weighed down by the destruction that trauma left behind, you are not destined to suffer and struggle forever. You don't have to be held down or held back by your past trauma any longer. I believe that it is absolutely possible for you to break those shackles, to become unbound.

**Scripture:**

**Psalms 30: 2**
***"Lord my God, I called to You for help, and You healed me."***

I'm going to show you how you can take the hard, rewarding steps toward healing that will enable you to live a more peaceful life. A more satisfying life. A more fulfilling life. A more joyful life. You can finally become the person you are meant to be, and for people of faith, you can become the person God has created you to be.

What Is Trauma?

So what is trauma anyway? Experts tell us that trauma is an event or series of events that are unwanted and unexpected, and we couldn't do anything to prevent them. Something happened that hurt us physically, emotionally, psychologically, even spiritually.

And when we don't deal with that trauma and it hangs around our lives unresolved, it leaves a deep imprint that can last for years, or most of our lives.

Well, I've got my own way of describing trauma. Getting struck by trauma is like getting hit by a bus. In my life, I've been hit by so many buses, it feels sometimes like some of them have backed up and run over me twice! Here's a list of some of the hits I have taken:

- Sexual abuse by male and female perpetrators as a young boy.
- Physical abuse combined with intimidating threats to keep me silent.
- Rejection and discrimination for being born half-black, half-white.
- Verbal and emotional abuse dumped on me by my high school basketball coach.
- The premature death of a child I never got to know.
- The tragic murder of my sister.
- Too many job and career losses and failures to count.
- A painful divorce that included getting pulverized by the legal and custody bias routinely thrown at men.
- A jolting diagnosis of cancer and, after battling through chemo, radiation and major surgery, dealing with the discovery that a completely different form of cancer was trying to invade a *new* part of my body.

Yep, that's a lot of buses. And I don't even like buses, not since I was a kid when I got stung by a swarm of bees that got loose in a bus driving people from our neighborhood to church one Sunday morning.

I could look at all those traumatic events and say, "Man, that really sucked" and then just put my head down and plod along, acting like none of those traumas happened or didn't really matter. Sometimes that's what I've tried to do. But somewhere along the way I made a decision: my life was not going to be dictated by all those crazy buses that knocked me off my feet. I was going to get up off my butt and do whatever it took to get better, to claim the life I was meant to live.

Now I'm here to share my experience with other men like you—and the women and men who deeply care about the hurting men in their lives. With all those traumas that piled up on top of me, and all the time I've devoted to climbing out of the rubble, I figure I've learned a few things about what trauma really looks and feels like, and what to do about it. I'm happy to pass that on. In the chapters ahead, I'll talk about the stuff men don't talk about, speaking from down in the trenches of the shame and pain of traumatic experiences and the destructive aftermath of trauma. And I'll shine the spotlight on a path that leads to healing, wellness and a whole new outlook on life.

**Scripture:**

**Proverbs 19:20 ESV**

***Listen to advice and accept instruction, so that you may gain wisdom in the future.***

The damage that trauma lays on us can take the form of addictions to alcohol, drugs, pornography, food, work or gambling. Or busted marriages and other failed relationships. Or jobs and careers that blow up or never get off the ground. Or major health issues and crises. Or bouts of violence and other criminal acts that land way too many men in prison. Or the constant cloud of sadness, depression or anxiety that leaves millions of men suffering in silence, to the point where many give up hope of ever living a satisfying life, or even turn to suicide. One way or another, trauma messes up our lives—until we deal with it.

**Biblical Insight:**

**A Biblical example of a man dealing with trauma**

God deals with a traumatized Elijah in 1 Kings 19. Note how God recognized Elijah's condition and what He did to restore Elijah.

**Story:**

**1 Kings 19:1-18 MSG**

*Ahab reported to Jezebel everything that Elijah had done, including the massacre of the prophets. Jezebel immediately sent a messenger to Elijah with her threat: "The gods will get you for this and I'll get even with you! By this time tomorrow you'll be as dead as any one of those prophets."*

*When Elijah saw how things were, he ran for dear life to Beersheba, far in the south of Judah. He left his young servant there and then went on into the desert for another day's journey. He came to a lone broom bush and collapsed in its shade, wanting in the worst way to be done with it all—to just die: "Enough of this, God! Take my life—I'm ready to join my ancestors in the grave!" Exhausted, he fell asleep under the lone broom bush.*

*Suddenly an angel shook him awake and said, "Get up and eat!"*

*He looked around and, to his surprise, right by his head were a loaf of bread baked on some coals and a jug of water. He ate the meal and went back to sleep. The angel of God came back, shook him awake again, and said, "Get up and eat some more—you've got a long journey ahead of you." He got up, ate and drank his fill, and set out. Nourished by that meal, he walked forty days and nights, all the way to the mountain of God, to Horeb. When he got there, he crawled into a cave and went to sleep. Then the word of God came to him:*

*"So Elijah, what are you doing here?"*

*"I've been working my heart out for the God-of-the-Angel-Armies," said Elijah. "The people of Israel have abandoned your covenant, destroyed the places of worship, and murdered your prophets. I'm the only one left, and now they're trying to kill me."*

*Then he was told, "Go, stand on the mountain at attention before God. God will pass by."*

*A hurricane wind ripped through the mountains and shattered the rocks before God, but God wasn't to be found in the wind; after the wind an earthquake, but God wasn't in the earthquake; and after the earthquake fire, but God wasn't in the fire; and after the fire a gentle and quiet whisper.*

*When Elijah heard the quiet voice, he muffled his face with his great cloak, went to the mouth of the cave, and stood there. A quiet voice asked, "So Elijah, now tell me, what are you doing here?" Elijah said it again, "I've been working my heart out for God, the God-of-the-Angel-Armies, because the people of Israel have abandoned your covenant, destroyed your places of worship, and murdered your prophets. I'm the only one left, and now they're trying to kill me."*

*God said, "Go back the way you came through the desert to Damascus. When you get there anoint Hazael; make him king over Aram. Then anoint Jehu son of Nimshi; make him king over Israel. Finally, anoint Elisha son of Shaphat from Abel Meholah to succeed you as prophet. Anyone who escapes death by Hazael will be killed by Jehu; and anyone who escapes death by Jehu will be killed by Elisha. Meanwhile, I'm preserving for myself seven thousand souls: the knees that haven't bowed to the god Baal, the mouths that haven't kissed his image."*

**Biblical Insight:**

**God recognizes trauma**

Elijah just finished slaughtering 450 prophets of Baal. Next, he gets a death threat from Jezebel, skips town, and buries himself where no one could find him. Physically exhausted and emotionally drained, he doesn't even want to live anymore and begs God to take his life. What does God do? He sends an angel to cook a very nutritious meal for him to replenish his physical body. God doesn't even bother to talk to Elijah until he is nourished and thoroughly rested. When Elijah's soul is restored, He then speaks to Elijah, reasons with him, and sends him on his next assignment.

God recognizes trauma. He understands that we are human and we are made of dust. He will restore us and prepare us so we can move on to our next assignment. God doesn't give up on us and we shouldn't give up on ourselves.

This book is divided into two parts. In Part 1, "Men Do Experience Trauma," I will zoom the camera in on a whole bunch of different traumas men encounter to help you see and better understand what trauma is. In Part 2, "Men Can Heal from Trauma," I'll take you inside the process of finally reaching out for help. I'll show you snapshots of the amazing possibilities waiting for you when you come to understand that the act of pursuing

Healing is not an act of weakness for men. It is absolutely a sign of strength!

Let me say that again: admitting to the need to get help when you've been plowed over by one or more buses carrying the name "Trauma" on the front is not a sign of weakness, it's a sign of strength.

Every day, through my public presentations about how men can heal from trauma and my one-on-one talks with men who turn to me when they're struggling with unresolved trauma, I have the privilege of guiding men toward that discovery. The choice of whether to take that courageous first step to embark on a journey toward help and wholeness is up to them. Or, if they began walking that healing path but got stuck or lost along the way, the choice to forge onward is also theirs to make. Whenever I help move another man toward the starting gate or urge him onto the next leg of the journey, I feel a real sense of gratitude to be of service.

My hope is that by reading this book, you will feel supported, encouraged and inspired to make that choice to get help, or to keep seeking ways to get better. To begin to break free from the shackles. To become unbound.

**Scripture:**

**Galatians 5:1 MSG**

*Christ has set us free to live a free life. So take your stand! Never again let anyone put a harness of slavery on you.*

No matter how young or how old you may be, or what mishaps and craziness may be messing up your life today, I want you to know that you are not alone. If you know or suspect that you were sexually abused, I stand with you. If you suffered or witnessed physical abuse growing up, I'm in your corner. If you were ever emotionally or verbally abused, I'm right here. If you've been rejected for who you are or who you're not, or you were abandoned or neglected by parents who weren't there physically or who had checked out with alcohol or drugs, pornography or workaholism, whatever it was, I've got your back. If you survived combat but still suffer the effects, or you've been knocked down or beat up by people and circumstances that you didn't want or expect, I encourage you to believe that you can change your course. Whether your problems show up in the form of losing a multimillion-dollar business, a long-term marriage, or your freedom by landing in prison or the prison of shame, you have the opportunity to heal. Starting today.

I don't know what bus or buses ran you over. Your story might sound very different from mine—I sure wouldn't wish all my traumas on anybody, and I wouldn't want you to compare my trauma to yours. Any trauma or loss that knocked you down or held you back is important to you, and it's calling out for your attention. Anyone can take those courageous steps toward healing.

If you picked up this book not so much as a trauma survivor but rather as a loved one of a male that you care about who has experienced trauma, I welcome you along, too. You will be making a major contribution to the life of that man or boy in your life just by handing them this book. You can let him know that if and when he chooses to share what he gained from reading it, you'll be right there to listen and support him.

And if you decide to read the book yourself, my hope is that what you learn about men and trauma will help you better understand the man you love and what he may be going through. Of course, it will be helpful for you to keep in mind that this is a book written more as a conversation from one guy (me) to hundreds or thousands of other guys. That's the channel you'll be tuning into. At times it may sound really different from your own experience, perspective and understanding. It's my intention to write a book for and about men and their struggles with trauma because while there may be a large number of written resources for women facing trauma, the unfortunate reality is that there are very few similar resources for men. I'm hoping to help fill that void.

**Biblical Insight:**

**A Biblical example of a Centurion who dealt with trauma**

There are many incidences of men and women facing trauma in the Bible. But I want to zoom in on a man, a centurion, a mighty Roman officer who was hit with trauma, an event he had no control over that invaded his life. Some commentators say the servant in this story was his child. Soldiers were not allowed to marry until age 50, but it would be common for soldiers to have a family without marriage. His loyal servant, possibly his son, was facing death and the centurion intervened on his behalf. Jesus rewarded the faith of the centurion by healing his servant.

**Story:**

**Luke 7:2-10 ESV**

*Now a centurion had a servant who was sick and at the point of death, who was highly valued by him. When the centurion heard about Jesus, he sent to him elders of the Jews, asking him to come and heal his servant. And when they came to Jesus, they pleaded with him earnestly, saying, "He is worthy to have you do this for him, for he loves our nation, and he is the one who built us our synagogue."*

*And Jesus went with them. When he was not far from the house, the centurion sent friends, saying to him, "Lord, do not trouble yourself, for I am not worthy to have you come under my roof. Therefore I did not presume to come to you. But say the word, and let my servant be healed. For I too am a man set under authority, with soldiers under me: and I say to one, 'Go,' and he goes; and to another, 'Come,' and he comes; and to my servant, 'Do this,' and he does it."*

*When Jesus heard these things, he marveled at him, and turning to the crowd that followed him, said, "I tell you, not even in Israel have I found such faith." And when those who had been sent returned to the house, they found the servant well.*

If you have picked up this book because you're a professional caregiver who offers therapeutic guidance and support to men, I welcome you to the conversation as well. As a male trauma survivor, I've got a lot to say. I hope it will prove useful to you.

I don't have all the answers. I'm not a psychologist, although I've learned a ton from those who offer clinical guidance and I'll be sharing some of those lessons with you here. I will provide you with some of my own ideas in the hope that some of them may be of value to you on your own healing path. Throughout the book, I'll be sprinkling in "Understanding Trauma Reminders," "Healing Trauma Reminders" and "Insights for Loved Ones" to highlight important points. For this Christian version of *The Unbound Man*, I have added scriptures, stories from the Bible, biblical insights, and prayers throughout the book as well.

But I'm not an "expert." I can't give you some surefire solution to heal your trauma. I just want to give you the support, the encouragement and the inspiration to reach out for help from those who can provide you with professional guidance, or to seek the support of peer-led groups and other tools that can help you to get well, to rebuild your life. One step at a time.

My voice is that of a survivor. A highly informed survivor, you could say. Through my story, and the stories of other men who have been impacted by this world of trauma we all live in, I'm going to share plenty of real-life experiences and, hopefully, quite a bit of wisdom too.

So I invite you to take a walk with me down this journey of men's trauma and healing. You just might find the key to unlock the door that opens to a new way of understanding and experiencing this life we all get to lead.

**Scripture:**

*Proverbs 3:5 AMP*

*Trust in the Lord with all your heart and lean not on your own understanding.*

**Prayer:**

Father,

I will trust in You with all of my heart and I will not lean on my own understanding. In all of my ways I will acknowledge You and You will direct my paths. Christ has set me free to live a free life. I take my stand to be unbound and I will never let anyone put a harness of slavery on me again! In Jesus' name,

Amen.

# PART ONE
## MEN DO EXPERIENCE TRAUMA

# 1

## WHY IT'S SO HARD FOR MEN TO DEAL WITH TRAUMA

*"We feel we are weak, cowardly or over-emotional if we don't keep our emotions under control. Men can't cry."*

- Mike Lew, *Victims No Longer*

Men never ask for help. We've all heard that description of how men are wired. Maybe we've said it ourselves a time or two, or we've heard it spoken by some of the women in our lives, perhaps with a tsk-tsk shaking of the head. We may believe there's some truth to the generalization—maybe a lot of truth? Doesn't it seem like there's something inside of us that holds us back from asking for help when we have a problem, when we're lost, not just physically but emotionally, when we're hurting, when we're stuck, when we're angry about something or a whole bunch of things in our life and we don't know what the heck to do about it?

Henry David Thoreau once said, "The mass of men lead lives of quiet desperation." This was the author who found peace and meaning hanging out at Walden Pond back in the 1850s, and I think the point he was trying to make was that men don't have to suffer in emptiness and despair. Instead, they can begin to make changes that can fill their lives with what really matters. I think his words about leading lives of quiet desperation still ring true today for men who don't ask for help when they really, really need it. Especially men who have experienced some form of trauma or loss. They try to plug along in life as if everything is okay, but inside they are suffering silently, weighed down by invisible wounds.

Several years ago, I attended a conference for men led by Mike Lew, an expert on recovery from male childhood sexual abuse. Speaking to a group of male survivors, he mentioned that the average length of time between when a male suffers sexual abuse and when he disclosed his being abused was twenty-five years. Wow, twenty-five years! That's a pretty long time to wait to ask for help for something that makes a huge impact in almost every part of a guy's life, isn't it? How many broken relationships, divorces, addictions, and job and business losses could you have averted if you disclosed what happened to those who could help you many years earlier?

I thought about what Mike said, and I thought about all the men I've guided into taking their first steps to deal with all kinds of trauma. Then it hit me: waiting twenty-five years to ask for help probably is an estimate for how long it takes men to deal with almost *any* trauma. Too many of us who have been struck by trauma wait and wait until the box of pain and the ways we try to hide from it gets so full that it feels like it's going to burst.

So what's up with that? What's so hard about dealing with trauma that makes men wait a quarter of a century to ask for help, if they ever ask for help at all? And what do men who have survived trauma and loss need to do to find the courage to ask for help—not twenty-five years later but right *now*?

To answer that question, I'll begin by taking a look at other generalizations about men. I'll share a bunch of statements about men, then tell you why they're not true. Whenever I talk to men and women about helping men heal, one of my roles is to be a myth buster. I present a bunch of these false truths about men, talk about why so many people believe them, then reveal the truth. Boom! The myth gets shattered. Here are a few of those common myths:

- **Men don't experience trauma.** (That's the biggest myth right there. I mean, why would we need to heal from trauma if we don't really experience it in the first place, right?)
- **Men don't experience the pain of loss.**
- **Men don't really hurt, because they are so strong. Men aren't victims of traumatic events such as sexual or physical abuse; they only create victims of abuse. Men overcome problems by simply sucking it up and moving on.**
- **Men don't feel.**
- **Men aren't really vulnerable.**

There are many ways to debunk myths like these and other false assumptions about men. One way is to call upon a few surprising statistics. (Sources for these statistics are noted at the end of this book.)

- Sixty-one percent of males have experienced at least one traumatic event in their lives.
- Ten percent of males have experienced *four or more* types of trauma. For better or worse, I'm a member of that club!
- Thirty percent of men were physically abused as boys. One in six males have experienced sexual abuse.
- Forty-one percent of domestic violence victims are men. Seventy-nine percent of suicide victims are males.

Statistics will always vary, depending on who's doing the research and how they conduct it. Also, it's always hard to pin down the numbers related to men and trauma because so many men go through their whole lives never revealing their traumas. They just hold on to their secrets. Those of us out there on the frontlines urging men to get the help they need to deal with trauma are left to fill in our own idea of what's really true. But those statistics offer some evidence that men really do experience trauma—much more than most people would imagine.

## You Are Not Alone

A while ago I was attending a recovery retreat, a mixed group of men and women focused on men doing work around trauma, when a licensed clinician led a simple exercise. He invited everyone to gather in a circle.

"Take a step forward if you or any male you know was physically abused as child," he said. Several people stepped forward.

"Now take a step forward if you or any male you know was sexually abused as a child," he continued. Again, some group members advanced one step.

"Take a step forward if you or any male you have known has been verbally abused," he said next. The exercise went on that way: "Take a step forward if you know any male who committed suicide" and "Take a step forward if you know any male who has been diagnosed with cancer." Each time, the men and women in the group who stepped forward were able to look around and discover firsthand just how prevalent male trauma really is.

**Insight for Loved Ones: You may be able to link one or more of these experiences to one or many men in your life. If as a loved one, you notice that he is in pain, you may be able to move him toward action to learn more.**

## Scripture:

### Matthew 9:35,36 TLB

*Jesus traveled around through all the cities and villages of that area, teaching in the Jewish synagogues and announcing the Good News about the Kingdom. And wherever he went he healed people of every sort of illness. And what pity he felt for the crowds that came, because their problems were so great and they didn't know what to do or where to go for help. They were like sheep without a shepherd.*

So, if you have been hit by one or more of those or other trauma buses, you are not alone. Men and boys get blindsided by traumatic events every day. Men and boys suffer. Men and boys hurt. Did you know that the third leading cause of death for boys is suicide?

Yet, with all this trauma going on, men only make up about one third of all mental health patients. But check the percentages of males and females in prison and you'll find that about ninety percent are males. About the same percentage of homicides are committed by males. For far too many boys and men, the pent-up pain and hurt from trauma, left unaddressed, spills over into acts of violence against others . . . or themselves.

If you walk into almost any Alcoholics Anonymous or Narcotics Anonymous meeting, you'll probably notice that most of the attendees are men. When you survey homeless people, you'll find that a huge majority of them are men.

Okay, let's take a minute to sort through all these numbers. Men and boys are traumatized at a high rate, but men and boys don't show up in big numbers at places where professionals can help them deal with trauma and its devastating effects on their lives. Men *do* show up big-time in prison, where most of them are probably acting out of the pain and suffering from unresolved trauma inflicted on them. And men stumble into addictions to alcohol or drugs, not to mention porn, at astronomical rates, because they're trying to numb themselves from all that pain they're carrying around from that unaddressed and unresolved trauma.

> **Insight for Loved Ones: There's a saying: "Hurting people hurt people." In my role with the cause to help men heal, I want to acknowledge that loved ones might well have been hurt and maybe are continuing to be hurt by our response to our trauma.**

So, what's going on with all these numbers? What does it mean for any man who knows or wonders if trauma has left its big, dark footprint on his life? It means we've got some work to do, to bust some other myths about men. We've got to extend our arms and sweep aside generalizations that just don't get us where we need to go to live peaceful and fulfilling lives.

## The Devastating Cost of "Manning Up"

"You gotta man up!" As boys and men, we hear this expression or some variation of it all the time.

"You're not really hurt; you've just got to man up and keep going." "No time to worry about that, just man up and deal."

Manning up, sucking it up, or any way you name it is the opposite of asking for help. It's part of the code of being a man that most of us are trained to follow from the time we are boys.

You just endure all the tough stuff that happens to you, whether it's the pain of being hit by your father at home or by the bully on the playground or school bus. Or getting hurt on the football field. Or living in a home where the adults abandon or neglect you, or shame and ridicule you all the time, or numb out with alcohol or drugs.

Manning up means never acknowledging any pain, which may explain why men don't get health problems checked out, often until real damage has been done. I can't bend my fingers all the way today because when I was playing basketball as a teenager, I didn't do the rehab exercises to heal them—I was in too much of a hurry to get back out on the court.

Manning up means not being weak. Manning up means denying your needs. Manning up means doing it all by yourself. Manning up means doing what you're supposed to do to conform to the way boys and men are supposed to think and act.

Manning up also means getting as many girls as you can. When I was playing sports in high school, I remember sitting around with the jocks on Monday mornings listening to guys bragging about the girls they "got something from" over the weekend. They used to pitch me crap if I didn't share my exploits from the weekend.

We live in a culture that may be changing in some ways when it comes to gender roles, but it's slow to change in other ways. Many of us grew up in places where rigid definitions of what it means to be a boy or a man still rule the land. I'll tell you what I was taught about being a man, and you can see how that compares to your own training. From my dad and the men and boys around me, I learned that being a man meant something like this:

Be tough. Be strong. Be aggressive. Be stoic. Never, ever cry (except after losing a big game in sports, the rare exception to this rule that boys and men are granted!) Be responsible. Be a provider. Make as much money as you can. Work harder than the guys around you. Be the best. Win. Get as much sex as you can from as many girls and women as possible because, as my dad would say, "Once you get married, you only get it one way."

Not long ago I watched the documentary *The Mask You Live In,* and I found myself nodding my head at other definitions that males in the movie were taught to live by:

- Never admit it when you're sad.
- Dominate the people around you.
- Get bigger and faster than the other guys.
- Don't talk about your feelings to anyone.
- When you can't work out a problem or disagreement with someone, just pretend there's no conflict. Or deal with it through violence.

That last message may partly explain the high rate of murders and assaults committed by men. For many males, the one emotion they are allowed to express their anger. All the other emotions, especially the more vulnerable feelings like sadness or fear, are off the table.

Men will tell you that feelings just get in the way of thinking anyway. And we should be able to think our way through any difficult feeling that might be creeping up, right?

**Scripture:**

**Matthew 11:28-30 MSG**

*"Are you tired? Worn out? Burned out on religion? Come to me. Get away with me and you'll recover your life. I'll show you how to take a real rest. Walk with me and work with me— watch how I do it. Learn the unforced rhythms of grace. I won't lay anything heavy or ill-fitting on you. Keep company with me and you'll learn to live freely and lightly."*

## Deny, Pretend, Delay

So, if you believe you must stick to these kinds of definitions of being a man, you learn how to hide what you feel. You don't talk about your feelings to other people, whether they are adults who might be able to do something about you carrying those feelings or other boys who would mock you for having them. You sure don't *show* those feelings to anyone, in any way, at any time. You just put on the mask of being cool, of being in control, of being unaffected by stuff that makes other people feel all kinds of feelings. You keep your head down. You don't stop and look behind you, and whenever anybody asks you how you are, you are quick to proclaim, "I'm good."

You can't show vulnerability because that would make you look weak or insecure. You would leave yourself wide open to being called all kinds of damaging, hurtful names. I spend a lot of time talking to men transitioning to life out of prison, encouraging them to get help for the wounds left by their traumas so they don't wind up back in jail, and I hear over and over from them that showing any sign of weakness in prison can literally get you killed.

If you buy into these definitions of being a man and you suffer trauma, you're in a bind. You hear those voices telling you that you're not supposed to have feelings, you can't be vulnerable, you should be in control, you need to man up. Ten you do what far too many men do, at least at first, after they have been knocked down by one of those trauma buses:

- **You deny.**

"Nothing really happened." "That didn't affect me." "That was so long ago, it doesn't matter now."

- **You minimize.**

"The abuse only went on for a while." "Maybe I just dreamed it." "I got hit, but I never had to go to the hospital." "I didn't want my mom to die from cancer, but that's just the way things go."

- **You pretend.**

"That wasn't abuse, it was just messing around." "I'm not shell shocked, I just can't sleep sometimes." "Sure, I got totally screwed in divorce court, but I've got a new girlfriend now."

- **You delay.**

"Maybe I should ask somebody about why I feel so depressed all the time, but I'm too busy with work stuff." "I can't talk about when I was sexually abused as a kid until I get old enough to understand all that psychological stuff." "It hurt when my business went under and my wife left me, but I've got to focus on building up the next business right now."

Sometimes men just rationalize away the problems left behind by unresolved trauma, or choose some way to avoid dealing with it. We say, "Yeah, that sucks, but it's time to get back to that work project." We power through. We keep on pushing. But we feel so isolated, so alone.

We often try to outrun the pain and shame by throwing ourselves into the quest for success through wealth, fame, prestige or reputation. Yet as hard as we try to outrun it, we're going to face the day when the pain, shame and other effects of not dealing with trauma catch up to us.

We've been looking at why it's so hard for us as men to deal with trauma. Now we need to bring in the wider consequences of not dealing with trauma and loss. As we've mentioned, men with unresolved trauma often wind up addicted to alcohol or drugs, or they stumble into one of those non-physical addictions to things like porn, or work, or food, or gambling or gaming. After I finally made the decision to deal with my trauma, I discovered three addictions of my own, which I'll tell you more about later. Basically, I grabbed whatever I could to numb myself from the pain and avoid facing what was really making me suffer.

**Biblical Insight:**

**A biblical example of Deny, Minimize, Pretend, and Delay**

There was a General in the army of Aram named Naaman. He denied that leprosy was in the way of his great success. He minimized his condition by keeping it under wraps from the general public. Only his wife, servants, and the king knew of his leprosy. Otherwise, the men would not have been anywhere near him. He pretended to be superior in stature to his servants and to the Hebrews. He despised the fact that he would have to bathe in the River Jordan, mostly used by the Hebrew people. In reality, he would be considered defiled, one of the dregs of society. He delayed his healing because of his pride and had to be convinced to 'lower' himself because he had nothing to lose.

Story:

## 2 Kings 5 MSG

*Naaman was general of the army under the king of Aram. He was important to his master, who held him in the highest esteem because it was by him that GOD had given victory to Aram: a truly great man, but afflicted with a grievous skin disease. It so happened that Aram, on one of its raiding expeditions against Israel, captured a young girl who became a maid to Naaman's wife. One day she said to her mistress, "Oh, if only my master could meet the prophet of Samaria, he would be healed of his skin disease."*

*Naaman went straight to his master and reported what the girl from Israel had said.*

*"Well then, go," said the king of Aram. "And I'll send a letter of introduction to the king of Israel."*

*So he went off, taking with him about 750 pounds of silver, 150 pounds of gold, and ten sets of clothes.*

*Naaman delivered the letter to the king of Israel. The letter read, "When you get this letter, you'll know that I've personally sent my servant Naaman to you; heal him of his skin disease."*

*When the king of Israel read the letter, he was terribly upset, ripping his robe to pieces. He said, "Am I a god with the power to bring death or life that I get orders to heal this man from his disease? What's going on here? That king's trying to pick a fight, that's what!"*

*Elisha the man of God heard what had happened, that the king of Israel was so distressed that he'd ripped his robe to shreds. He sent word to the king, "Why are you so upset, ripping your robe like this? Send him to me so he'll learn that there's a prophet in Israel."*

*So Naaman with his horses and chariots arrived in style and stopped at Elisha's door.*

*Elisha sent out a servant to meet him with this message: "Go to the River Jordan and immerse yourself seven times. Your skin will be healed and you'll be as good as new."*

*Naaman lost his temper. He spun around saying, "I thought he'd personally come out and meet me, call on the name of God, wave his hand over the diseased spot, and get rid of the disease. The Damascus rivers, Abana and Pharpar, are cleaner by far than any of the rivers in Israel. Why not bathe in them? I'd at least get clean." He stomped off, mad as a hornet.*

*But his servants caught up with him and said, "Father, if the prophet had asked you to do something hard and heroic, wouldn't you have done it? So why not this simple 'wash and be clean'?"*

*So he did it. He went down and immersed himself in the Jordan seven times, following the orders of the Holy Man. His skin was healed; it was like the skin of a little baby. He was as good as new.*

*He then went back to the Holy Man, he and his entourage, stood before him, and said, "I now know beyond a shadow of a doubt that there is no God anywhere on earth other than the God of Israel.*

**Biblical Insight:**

**God recognizes trauma**

God wants us to unmask our trauma by admitting the addiction, realizing the massive damage it is causing to ourselves and others, facing reality, and running to Him to get the healing we so desperately need.

> **Insight for Loved Ones:** The addictions that mask our trauma can be incredibly damaging to those who love us. As one example, I've spent time with many partners suffering the devastating effects of pornography addiction on relationships.

Men carrying the burden of unresolved trauma are also more likely to become sad or depressed, to find themselves failing at work and in relationships, to experience low self-esteem, to act out their anger in violent or manipulative acts. Some traumas leave behind a trail of nightmares, flashbacks of a high level of fear and anxiety. Or they lead to compulsive behavior, or extreme distrust of people and life. Even for survivors of trauma who do become "successful" as measured by money or title, from the inside their lives still suck.

> **Understanding Trauma Reminder:** According to the World Health Organization, depression is the leading cause of disability worldwide. If you have any symptoms related to depression, share them with a medical professional, even if you don't believe they are linked to trauma.

Men struggling with all these kinds of symptoms usually don't connect their problems with trauma. That discovery comes much later, after the choice to pursue healing—to get help.

**Biblical Insight:**

**A Bible lesson on leadership**

God has great compassion for those who are traumatized and expects the spiritually healthy to assist in their recovery.

**Story:**

**Ezekiel 34:1-9 MSG**

*God's Message came to me: "Son of man, prophesy against the shepherd-leaders of Israel. Yes, prophesy! Tell those shepherds, 'God, the Master, says: Doom to you shepherds of Israel, feeding your own mouths! Aren't shepherds supposed to feed sheep? You drink the milk, you make clothes from the wool, you roast the lambs, but you don't feed the sheep. You don't build up the weak ones, don't heal the sick, don't doctor the injured, don't go after the strays, don't look for the lost. You bully and badger them. And now they're scattered every which way because there was no shepherd—scattered and easy pickings for wolves and coyotes. Scattered—my sheep!—exposed and vulnerable across mountains and hills. My sheep scattered all over the world, and no one out looking for them!*

*'Therefore, shepherds, listen to the Message of God: As sure as I am the living God — Decree of God, the Master — because my sheep have been turned into mere prey, into easy meals for wolves because you shepherds ignored them and only fed yourselves...'"*

## Women Suffer from Our Unresolved Trauma

Men dealing with these issues, or trying to avoid dealing with them, assume that the only one suffering is them. As I highlighted in an Insight for Loved Ones earlier in this chapter, they're wrong. The truth is, when we try to power through while carrying a big chunk of unresolved trauma on our shoulders, our loved ones suffer, too. I've been saying for many years with little to no pushback that much of the trauma that women experience comes directly from traumatized men projecting their trauma onto them.

How else does our trauma impact our loved ones? They suffer when we numb out or try to outrun the pain, because we're not present in our relationships. We neglect, abandon or mistreat our partners. Our marriages or relationships fall apart, or our partners issue us ultimatums: "This has to change or I'm gone."

Those close to us are also impacted when we suffer financial or vocational loss or failure because of the impact of trauma. For some men, anger spills over into violence they inflict on those whom they insist they love. In ways large and small, many men have projected their trauma onto women or other loved ones through hurtful and harmful acts.

Sometimes they just get sad witnessing the pain and distress burdening the men they love. They feel powerless to help them begin to face whatever is really bothering them. And that "whatever it is" is usually the effects of trauma. When a man goes to the extreme of committing suicide, he may end his own suffering but the loved ones he leaves behind have to carry all the baggage of his unresolved trauma.

When we're wrestling with unresolved trauma, our partners suffer. So do our children and our entire families, and our friends and colleagues. And when you consider the cost of violence or addiction, you could say that society suffers too.

**Scripture:**

**1 Timothy 5: 7, 8 MSG**

*Tell these things to the people so that they will do the right thing in their extended family. Anyone who neglects to care for family members in need repudiates the faith. That's worse than refusing to believe in the first place.*

**Insight for Loved Ones: When you support or help the traumatized male in your life, you're also helping yourself.**

Still, in the fallout from the unresolved trauma that you try to bear silently, the one who hurts the most is you. For many men, the impact may surface in ways more subtle than alcoholism or bankruptcy. You simply can't enjoy your life the way you want to.

When I was carrying the weight of unresolved trauma from sexual abuse, I couldn't experience the joy of a sunset or a ride on a roller coaster. If I went to the beach, I couldn't sink into that wonderful sensation of feeling sand on my bare feet because I wouldn't let myself take my shoes off. I was living in shackles because I had linked pleasure with shame, which distorted my thinking into a state where something that was "good" was really "bad."

**Scripture:**

**Proverbs 9:3-6 MSG**

*Lady Wisdom goes to town, stands in a prominent place, and invites everyone within the sound of her voice: "Are you confused about life, don't know what's going on? Come with me, oh come, have dinner with me! I've prepared a wonderful spread—fresh-baked bread, roast lamb, and carefully selected wines. Leave your impoverished confusion and live! Walk up the street to a life with meaning."*

## Breaking Free

It was only after I made the courageous choice to pursue healing from my many traumas that I could soak in some of those simple joys and pleasures, and I'm still working on it. That. That path also steered me into breaking free from my addictions. It guided me to a place where I could actually enter into and maintain a healthy relationship. It led me to make the decision to devote my life's work to helping men heal, to find the strength to address their traumas and seek the help they need to rebuild their lives.

To turn down that path and stay on it, I had to come to grips with my own beliefs about being a man. Over time, one by one, I slid some of those rigid definitions to the side and replaced them with definitions more aligned with my primary goal: to stop hitting the self-destruct button in my life!

If I was going to get better, I had to accept the idea that asking for and receiving help is totally natural, not to mention healthy. As you will see later in the book, I started asking for help so often and so easily that I put together a whole big team of helpers in my life. I came to adopt new truths about being a man:

- Feelings are natural to have and to express.

- You can be vulnerable and still be strong.

- Trying to man up and power through pain and problems just creates more pain and problems; acknowledging those hurts is the first step in overcoming them.

- Trying to numb ourselves from our suffering just doesn't work and can destroy our life, as well as the lives of others connected to us.

- Talking about what's bothering me doesn't make me less of a man, it makes me healthier as a person.

- Going to the doctor regularly, caring for my physical health, is a strength not a weakness.

> **Insight for Loved Ones:** I have tried to help break these stereotypes with my sons by encouraging and praising them when they cry or show vulnerability, or by gently asking, "What are you feeling?" or "How do you feel about that?"

So, I made lots of changes in my beliefs, but let's be clear here: I still really, *really* like being a guy! I didn't throw out all the traditional understandings about men and sign on to some squeaky clean, politically correct, gender neutral definition. No way. And I'm sure not going to tell you that you have to do that either.

As you seek to turn onto the path of healing from your trauma and loss, you'll decide what it means for you to be a man in a way that supports and encourages healing and wholeness. Like some of the men I know who have gotten better after living so long with unresolved trauma, you will slowly let go of or reshape some of those beliefs you used to accept without question. You may discover that living in a tight box of masculinity is too suffocating. Breaking out of that box and making your own choices about a code to live by could help give you the strength to face whatever trauma or loss you experienced.

## Scripture:

## Romans 12: 1, 2 TLB

*And so, dear brothers, I plead with you to give your bodies to God. Let them be a living sacrifice, holy—the kind he can accept. When you think of what he has done for you, is this too much to ask? Don't copy the behavior and customs of this world, but be a new and different person with a fresh newness in all you do and think. Then you will learn from your own experience how his ways will really satisfy you.*

## Trauma Has No Boundaries

We as men do hurt. We have been wounded by others, a list that may include our dads and moms, our siblings, our uncles and aunts, grandfathers, cousins, spouses or partners, teachers or coaches, bullies, priests or other clergy, bosses or co-workers, and many more.

Trauma is real. It can show up at your doorstep at any time, in any life situation. It doesn't matter how old you are, what work you do, how much money you make, or how many years of education you completed. It doesn't matter where you live or who lives with you. It doesn't matter if you're a person or faith, or have no specific faith at all.

Trauma has no age boundaries, no cultural boundaries, no socioeconomic boundaries. Most of the guys who seek my help in dealing with the impact of trauma are men of wealth and influence. Contrary to the myth that only the down-and-out suffer trauma, I have more meetings with men in upscale athletic, golf and country clubs than I ever do at McDonald's.

What we do, what title we hold, what we know, what car we drive, what we can afford, or who we can impress will never fill the empty crater in our hearts or empty those dark closets in our lives left behind by unaddressed, unresolved trauma. Rich or poor, young or old, light skin or dark skin, mansion or prison cell—if you have been hurt by trauma, you are definitely not alone.

You've been hearing about how that's true, and the challenges we as men face in dealing with trauma. Now, as we continue along the trail of Part 1, you'll be *seeing* trauma inflicted on men and witnessing the deep imprint it leaves behind.

As I share the details of these stories, the picture may not look pretty at times. I try to tell it like it really is for me, to be authentic, so that you may see yourself in those stories and know that somebody else gets it—and gets you. I invite you to read only what fits for you and leave the rest. Then, in Part 2, I'll help you see and *feel* what it's like to walk down that path of healing, to break the shackles and build a more satisfying and fulfilling life.

Okay, let's zoom the camera in on some of those trauma buses.

**Scripture:**

**2 Corinthians 10:3-6 MSG**

*The world is unprincipled. It's dog-eat-dog out there! The world doesn't fight fair. But we don't live or fight our battles that way—never have and never will. The tools of our trade aren't for marketing or manipulation, but they are for demolishing that entire massively corrupt culture. We use our powerful God-tools for smashing warped philosophies, tearing down barriers erected against the truth of God, fitting every loose thought and emotion and impulse into the structure of life shaped by Christ. Our tools are ready at hand for clearing the ground of every obstruction and building lives of obedience into maturity.*

**Prayer:**

Father,

I give my body to You. I choose to be a living sacrifice, holy—the kind You can accept. I will not copy the behavior and customs of this world but choose to be a different person with a fresh newness in all I do and think. I will learn from my own experience how Your ways will really satisfy me. In Jesus' name,

Amen.

## 2

## MEN EXPERIENCE SEXUAL TRAUMA— FROM OTHER MALES

> *"Ashamed, humiliated and confused, you figured there was no one you could talk to and confide in for help. Who would believe you anyway?"*
>
> \- Michael S. Figgers, *Healing the Hearts of Broken Men*

Many people assume that most perpetrators of sexual abuse are strangers. In reality, that's just another myth. Because when it comes to sexual abuse of female or male children, 90 percent of the abusers are known to the child.

These are usually people whom the survivors of abuse not only know but trust: a parent or step-parent, a grandparent, an aunt or uncle, an older cousin, a brother-in-law. Perpetrators may be other trusted adults or adolescents: a teacher, a clergy member, a babysitter. It's a sad statement about the world we live in that people who are entrusted with the care and well-being of children wind up inflicting harm on their bodies, their minds, their hearts and their souls. Over and over again, trust is violated. Trauma invades the lives of a child in a way that leaves long-lasting, invisible wounds.

As we revealed in the previous chapter, sexual abuse is not something that only happens to girls. One in six males are sexually abused in their lives. The rates for females are usually estimated as one in four, but some professionals dedicated to helping men heal will tell you that the rate for boys may be in the same range as girls.

Yes, millions of men really do experience sexual trauma. Males, like females, have their trust violated, with devastating effects that torment them all through childhood and into their adult lives.

## My Ideal Babysitter

When I was seven years old, I really liked my older cousin Jimmy. He was a big part of one of the best times of my life to that point. It was the summer between my first and second grade and my parents, who almost never took us on vacations, treated me to a whole week at a large state park. As an only child, I was always hungry for playmates, and even though Jimmy was several years older than me, maybe thirteen or fourteen, he was willing to hang out with me for hours at a time. This park was full of recreational opportunities for kids. So we swam. We played ping-pong. We bounced on the trampoline. He showed me how to play pool. By the end of that vacation, I thought Jimmy was the best cousin anyone could ever ask for.

When the following summer rolled around, my parents knew they would need a babysitter for me during the long days when they both worked, my mom as an assistant vice president of a bank and my dad as a foreman at a steel mill.

"Can Jimmy be my babysitter?" I asked. They had hired a sitter for me the previous summer, and although I do not have any specific memories of what happened, I vaguely sensed that she did something sexually inappropriate to me. I sure didn't want her back again. After some discussion between my mom and dad, and further talks with Jimmy's mom and dad, it was decided. Yes, I could have Jimmy as my babysitter.

In fact, not only would my older cousin take care of me during the day while my parents worked, he would stay overnight at our house in northeast Portland during the week, before going home to his family on weekends. Jimmy would even be able to sleep in my bedroom, in the bed right next to mine.

"This is going to be great!" I said to myself, remembering all my fun with Jimmy on that vacation and imagining how much *more* fun it was going to be to have him around for the whole summer. We would play together. We'd walk to the Dairy Queen. I'd introduce Jimmy to my friends, who would be impressed and jealous that a boy that much older would be hanging around me. They mostly had *girl* babysitters, and they probably weren't much fun. Unfortunately, my image of how it was going to be would turn out to be the extreme opposite of reality.

(A word of caution here, especially for male readers who have survived any form of sexual abuse: you may find some of the following detailed accounts of what happened to me with my cousin to be disturbing. I urge you to do whatever you need to do to feel safe as you decide how to proceed.)

The betrayal began on the very first day of summer vacation, my first day alone with Jimmy. It was still early in the morning and I was just lying there in my bed when my cousin came over. Right away, he began touching me in my private parts.

"You like that, don't you?" he asked.

"Uh, um, I don't know," I mumbled, too confused and jolted by what was happening to know what the right answer was.

"Oh, yeah, you do," Jimmy answered. Then he started to pinch and grab me, with a force that took my breath away. It was like he was trying to communicate a message something like this: *Whether you say you like it or not, it doesn't matter, because I'm going to keep touching you until I'm done with you, and there's nothing you can do about it.*

It didn't take my cousin long to go beyond just touching me. He soon proceeded to make me touch *him* in his private parts. He made me participate in many sexual acts—I don't need to tell you exactly what they were. Right from that first time, I felt humiliated and degraded. And totally crushed. This was the cousin I was going to have fun with, the older and more mature boy who would take care of me. This was the person I had *picked* to be my babysitter!

**Scripture:**

**Psalm 41:9 NLT**

***Even my best friend, the one I trusted completely, the one who shared my food, has turned against me.***

A Summer in Hell

As that first week went on, my cousin made it known that this abuse was not going to be an isolated event. Not even close. He was going to be touching me and doing things to me, and making me touch him and do things to him, just about every day. Over and over he would force me to go "there."

Jimmy was always smart enough to stop what he was doing to me at least a half-hour before my parents would get home, to avoid getting caught. But as time went on, he was not content with only abusing me during those hours when the coast was clear because my parents were of at work or out on a shopping run. After all, he was sleeping in the same bedroom with me, upstairs in a converted attic space. Far from my parents' room downstairs.

Since Jimmy was older than me, he got to stay up later at night. He would watch TV down in the basement, the place I no longer dared to go because it felt even more scary and dangerous than my room. When he finally came upstairs to go to bed, I would already be asleep. When I woke up, he would be on top of me, and before I could even react, he would shove a pillow over my head and push my face down into the mattress with so much pressure I could hardly breathe. I couldn't move either, and if I tried to scream, not that I could with my face buried, I knew without a doubt that he would kill me. Right then, right there.

Once again, my cousin used me to fulfill some kind of twisted desire. Once again, his violating sexual contact would be accompanied by grabbing and pinching, delivering another whole layer of pain and hurt while keeping me under his control.

After a while, my cousin added another wrinkle to his control scheme. One night, after leaving me to finally fall off to sleep, my body hurting almost everywhere, he leaned in very close to me and said in a voice just above a whisper, "If you tell anyone, I will kill you." Not for one moment did I question whether he meant it.

And that's the way the summer between second and third grade unfolded. When my cousin wasn't abusing me sexually, he was finding other ways to torture, torment and dominate me. He liked to give me the burns you get on your arms when somebody rubs them back and forth rapidly while twisting your skin. And he would take special pleasure in rolling up a bath towel, getting it good and wet, and then *thwack!* He'd get me on my arms, my legs, my back. His handiwork would leave welts all over my body. *Thwack! Thwack!* He'd get me on my face and then, lowering the towel, he would snap that wet towel right at my genitals.

The first time I cried during this wet towel bombardment, Jimmy shouted, "Sissy!" Then he pushed me outside, stark naked. I hid from the neighbors in the backyard. After a while, believing that my cousin had forgotten about me, I ran up to the side door. I figured I could sneak in and hide from him inside the house until my parents got home. But that was not going to happen. My cousin had locked the door, and as I tried to pry it open, he stood laughing at me through the windows.

When he finally let me back in, it was only to start punching and hurting me again. One time he hit me so hard I really thought I was going to die. The pain always came with more threats, and after a while those threats became so vicious, they hurt worse than the abuse. It felt like his words were ripping my soul right out of me.

> **Understanding Trauma Reminder: Treats and intimidation can cause pain and suffering as deep as the physical hurt.**

The only place where I could hide from my cousin and his horrors was the bathroom. The bathroom door locked from the inside, and he knew that if he broke the door down to get at me, he would have a lot of explaining to do with my parents. The problem was, I would have to sneak into the bathroom when my cousin wasn't watching me or he would just hold open the door until I was finished. Even when I was able to reach my fortress without him, he would pound on the door so loudly and for so long that sometimes I just gave up. Or I would just get scared being alone in there for hours and voluntarily surrender my safe haven. Once I stepped outside the bathroom, he would immediately hit me. And touch me. And more.

**Insight for Loved Ones: It's helpful to understand that many survivors of male sexual or physical trauma only feel safe in rooms that have doors they can shut, or, even better, doors that lock.**

These sexual assaults continued in a familiar pattern. Each time, I would feel varying degrees of fear, pain, humiliation and confusion. But something else would emerge from time to time: a sexual response on my part. It felt like my body was betraying me. Tis totally confused me, adding to my shame. It wasn't until I was well along in my healing journey as an adult that I learned that I was having a totally natural physiological response. And it didn't change the picture: what was going on was abuse, plain and simple.

One of the few things that would get my cousin to briefly pause in his campaign of terror involved a neighbor. The girl next door would keep her blinds open when she took off her clothes, and Jimmy would stop to watch her. Sometimes he'd force me to watch with him. Then, with more sexual images to draw upon, he would turn his attention back to me.

Occasionally, my cousin allowed me to go outside on my own to play. He was smart enough to know that when my parents got home from work and asked me what I did all day, and I said I never left the house, they might get suspicious. Sometimes the kids in our neighborhood, where our house was located on a popular corner, would knock on the door and ask if I could come out. My cousin knew that if I always said no, stories might start going around among their families. So I could actually go out and play a little kickball with my friends, or walk to the Dairy Queen three blocks away, or ride my bike a short distance. For those precious moments, I was safe from my abuser.

## Expanding His Circle of Abuse

Several weeks into the summer, my cousin told me to invite a couple of my friends over to our house to play with me. "No!" I said to myself. "I am not going to allow my cousin to do to my friends what he is doing to me."

I stalled, making any kind of excuse I could think of. But if I thought I could outlast my perpetrator, I was naïve. When I resorted to begging, he stared at me with that menacing look and said, "If you don't invite them over tomorrow, I'm going to kill Crystal." And with those words, he knew that he would get his way. Crystal, an all-white Alaskan Samoyed, was more than my dog. She was my confidant, my friend, my ally.

"Okay," I muttered. On that sweltering hot August day, I followed my cousin's order and invited my friends over for a water gun fght. When they arrived, we ran around the house squirting each other in our bathing suits.

"That must be fun," my cousin said. "Now why don't you just take of your bathing suits and shoot each other in your privates."

My two buddies looked confused.

"Oh, it's no big deal," my cousin insisted. "Watch, Matt and I will go first." Then he shot me that look a perpetrator gives his victim that communicates what will happen if his demands are not met. I did as I was instructed to do, and before long we were all naked shooting our water guns. That. That was only the first step in my cousin's devious plan.

Except something happened to sabotage that plan. One of my friends heard his mother calling him home and promptly put his bathing suit back on and left. Immediately, I turned to my other friend and said, "You better go now, too. Your mom will be calling any minute."

As soon as my cousin was alone with me, I got the welting of my life with the towel as punishment for letting my friends leave. That. That didn't stop me from telling all my friends the next day that my mom said that no one could come over my house when my parents weren't home. My mother never said any such thing, of course, but in the midst of this summer of terror, when I felt humiliated and powerless, I had at least summoned the strength to protect my friends. I had drawn a line.

**Scripture:**

**Psalm 82:4 NLT**

*Rescue the poor and helpless; deliver them from the grasp of evil people.*

A Plea to God

You may wonder whether I ever tried to ask for help. Did I ever dare tell my parents that the adolescent boy whose hands they had entrusted to deliver my care was sexually and physically abusing me? I did try to inform my parents of what was happening to me, which I will explain a little later. But before I tried to share it with them, I actually tried to ask someone I thought could do the most to come to my aid.

It was a weekday, but for some reason my cousin was out of the house briefly. I seized that moment to do something I had been wanting to do for weeks.

Standing in front of my bedroom mirror, tears streaming down my face, I sputtered, "God, please make it stop!" (Tough small, I was a consistent church-goer even at seven years old. My parents didn't attend church, but I'd grab the Sunday church bus to Holiday Park Church of God every Sunday.)

God did not make the abuse stop. Before that same day was over, my cousin had come back home and had me pinned down on my bed, my clothes in a messy heap on the floor, doing what he had been doing to me for two months. And what he would go on doing to me for a few more weeks of summer.

I didn't return to church for fifteen years after that, believing at the time that God did not protect me, that he had abandoned me, and that I was truly all alone.

**Scripture:**

**Matthew 18:6 MSG**

***But if you give them a hard time, bullying or taking advantage of their simple trust, you'll soon wish you hadn't. You'd be better off dropped in the middle of the lake with a millstone around your neck.***

Feeling more and more desperate, I would fantasize about trying to kill my cousin. I thought maybe I could poison him, but I had no earthly idea how. I didn't have the strength to kill him anyway. If I was going to have any hope at all, I needed an adult to intervene.

Tere had been one moment when I tried to describe to my mom that something was going on with my cousin that was not right. But somehow, as a seven-year-old who lacked the words for what was happening and who was under the intimidation of constant threats, my message did not get through.

**Understanding Trauma Reminder: Despite what you may believe at your core to be true, not being able to stop the abuse or tell anybody what was happening doesn't mean in any way that the abuse was your fault!**

My cousin had gotten good at manipulating things between me and my parents. One day, when my mom had taken us to the grocery store, he urged me to grab some candy and steal it. When I refused, he snatched the candy from me and marched toward the cash register. When we reached my mom, he said, "I caught Matt trying to steal this candy!" My mom believed my cousin. He was the older, more responsible boy. He was trustworthy. I was just a young kid who didn't know better. I later got a spanking from my dad, very much to my cousin's delight.

**Scripture:**

**Psalm 9:13-18 TLB**

*And now, O Lord, have mercy on me; see how I suffer at the hands of those who hate me. Lord, snatch me back from the jaws of death. Save me, so that I can praise you publicly before all the people at Jerusalem's gates and rejoice that you have rescued me... For the needs of the needy shall not be ignored forever; the hopes of the poor shall not always be crushed.*

Eventually, my mom must have had a few suspicions of her own that something just wasn't quite right with my cousin. About a week before summer vacation was over, she took me aside and gently asked me a question.

"So how is it working out with Jimmy? Do you like having him as your babysitter?"

"Well, um, I mean . . . no, not really," I finally mumbled.

Within a week, my cousin's bags were packed and he headed home for good. On the final day, when we were alone together in our bedroom, which was about to become *my* bedroom again, he leaned into me the way he had done countless times before, like some kind of monster trying to terrorize its victim.

"Remember what I said—if you ever tell your parents or anybody else, I will come find you. And I will kill you," he proclaimed, with his menacing stare, before going on. "You know what, Matt? *You* are a total waste, a zero. You hear me, Matt? You ain't never gonna amount to anything. Don't forget that." I didn't and have spent most of my life trying to prove him wrong and, at times, based on shattered self-esteem, trying to prove him right.

I didn't forget. My cousin's stinging words stuck with me for the next day, for the next week, for the next year. One way or another, they clung to my body and my being well into my adult life. Tere are times and situations where I still hear the echoes of my cousin's words today.

The scars from the kind of sexual trauma that I experienced are that deep, that powerful, that long-lasting.

## Biblical Insight:

### A biblical example of traumatized men, and of men causing trauma

Unfortunately, men experiencing sexual trauma from other men is as old as time. Not even male angels were safe. And God finds it deplorable.

## Story:

### Genesis 18:20, 21 AMP

*And the Lord said, "The outcry [of the sin] of Sodom and Gomorrah is indeed great, and their sin is exceedingly grave. I will go down now, and see whether they have acted [as vilely and wickedly] as the outcry which has come to Me [indicates]; and if not, I will know."*

## Biblical Insight:

### God hears our cries

A cry from earth reached the ears of God and was so alarming, that all the activity in heaven stopped. God dispatched His angels to investigate the accusations presented to Him.

## Story:

### Genesis 19:1-11 MSG

*The two angels arrived at Sodom in the evening. Lot was sitting at the city gate. He saw them and got up to welcome them, bowing before them and said, "Please, my friends, come to my house and stay the night. Wash up. You can rise early and be on your way refreshed."*

*They said, "No, we'll sleep in the street."*

*But he insisted, wouldn't take no for an answer; and they relented and went home with him. Lot fixed a hot meal for them and they ate.*

*Before they went to bed, men from all over the city of Sodom, young and old, descended on the house from all sides and boxed them in. They yelled to Lot, "Where are the men who are staying with you for the night? Bring them out so we can have our sport with them!"*

*Lot went out, barring the door behind him, and said, "Brothers, please, don't be vile! ...*

*They said, "Get lost! You drop in from nowhere and now you're going to tell us how to run our lives. We'll treat you worse than them!" And they charged past Lot to break down the door.*

*But the two men reached out and pulled Lot inside the house, locking the door. Then they struck blind the men who were trying to break down the door, both leaders and followers, leaving them groping in the dark.*

**Biblical Insight:**

**God saw Lot's trauma**

*Just living in this environment caused Lot great trauma and the Lord recognizes this as so. How much worse a trauma it is to actually experience the abuse!*

**Story:**

**2 Peter 2: 7-9 AMP**

*Lot, who was tormented by the immoral conduct of unprincipled and ungodly men (for that just man, while living among them, felt his righteous soul tormented day after day by what he saw and heard of their lawless acts), then [in light of the fact that all this is true, be sure that] the Lord knows how to rescue the godly from trial...*

## Abused Males Are Not Alone

Sexual abuse might not be a form of trauma that you ever experienced. If so, you certainly have something to be grateful for. But if you know or suspect that you did survive sexual abuse when you were a boy, I urge you to remember that you are not alone. I'm right here with you. So are thousands of other male survivors who care about the welfare of others whose lives have been damaged by the abuse at the hands of those they knew and trusted. We have learned that healing is possible, that with lots of help from professionals experienced in assisting male sexual abuse survivors, you really can face these demons.

You can rebuild your life. You can find peace and happiness. You can build fulfilling relationships, and a whole lot more. You don't need to hide yourself away in your pain and shame.

> **Insight for Loved Ones: If you are a woman or a man who experienced sexual trauma perpetrated by a man, you may not feel safe enough to hear your loved one share his own traumatic experience(s). You can still support him by guiding him to healing professionals.**

Even if you only sense that something may have happened, but you lack any specific memories of experiencing sexual abuse by another male, you can still reach out for help and embark on the road to healing. Tere's a phrase, often repeated in the circles of those who heal from male sexual trauma and those who guide them in that healing, that may help:

### *Just because you can't remember doesn't mean that nothing happened!*

What I have reported to you about my sexual abuse at the hands of my older cousin is not something I could recall in any detail for many, many years. I'll explain how those memories finally did come back to me and what I did about them later in this book.

Meanwhile, if this is not the kind of trauma that fts your experience, keep reading. We've got a lot more ground of male trauma to cover, and I'll be walking right alongside you every step of the way.

**Prayer:**

Father,

Have mercy on me. You see how I suffered at the hands of those who hate me. Snatch me back from the jaws of death. Save me, so that I can praise You. Give me reason to rejoice. Come to my rescue!

Please meet all my needs and fulfill all my hopes of deliverance. Unbind me from these chains of abuse. Bind up my broken heart and thoroughly heal all the layers of my wounded memories and emotions. I thank You and praise You for it! In Jesus' name,

Amen.

# 3

## MEN EXPERIENCE SEXUAL TRAUMA— FROM FEMALES TOO

*"Any act that arouses the abuser and makes the victim uncomfortable is sexual abuse."*

- Randy Boyd, *Healing the Man Within*

The impact of sexual trauma does not end when the abuse stops. Far from it. That. That trauma that many of us survived as boys continues to show up in our lives in dozens of ways, over the course of many years.

What happened with my older cousin was definitely still following me after that summer in hell ended and I went back to school for third grade. Being around the other kids, I felt dirty. It didn't matter that I had only been doing what I was forced to do by my cousin. I still felt ashamed, damaged.

Desperately in need of a kind, loving teacher, I found myself in the classroom of a teacher who would often resort to mean and demeaning tactics in dealing with her students. Yeah, she was a real witch. You know how when you're really good at something, immature classmates respond by calling you names that are exactly the opposite of how you are? Well, the other boys and girls in my class started calling me "Bird Brain," and she didn't do much to stop them. Before the bullying started, I had excelled in math. After their taunts got to me, I began struggling mightily in my favorite subject. Rather than showing any compassion or understanding of what was happening to me, my teacher began criticizing me.

At home, I was having trouble sleeping. Night after night, I would wake up in a nightmare. It was always the same horrible dream:

*A monster, the scariest monster my mind can imagine, is chasing me through my house. I run as fast as I can, and then run even faster. Somehow, I manage to stay barely out of the clutches of this monster. I keep running down the street, block after block, with the monster still chasing me, trying to catch me and devour me.*

*Finally, I run into a bowling alley. When I find myself in the middle of a bowling lane, I know that I am trapped. The monster has now turned into professional bowler Earl Anthony, and he suddenly picks up a bowling ball and throws it right at me. Because he is the number one bowler in the world, I know that his aim is absolutely true and that in an instant, I will be dead.*

*And I know that this monster is not really a world-famous bowler. It is my cousin, my abuser.*

Just before that bowling ball would strike me, I would wake up from the nightmare. Still terrified that the monster was chasing me and would find me, I would run downstairs, rush into my parents' bedroom, and climb into their bed. They would allow me to sleep with them the rest of the night.

I don't think my parents ever asked me what made me run into their bed like that, and I never volunteered the truth. The nightmare just kept recurring almost every day for a year before tapering to a couple of nights per month for a while and then popping up now and again all the way through my teenage years.

Sometime during third grade, however, I did find the nerve to tell my parents what Jimmy had done to me. I couldn't explain the details. It just came out in bits and pieces: "He hurt me . . . he touched me . . . he did bad things to me."

My mom and dad called a meeting with my aunt and uncle, Jimmy's parents. For some reason, they agreed to have this meeting in the parking lot of a bank located along one of the main roads through northeast Portland. I sat in our car while my cousin sat in his family's car, while the grown-ups met outside and talked.

When my parents retuned to our car, my dad announced, "You don't have to worry about this anymore." Not another word was said about it.

Well, at least I had some assurance that my cousin would not come back as my babysitter again. But this little meeting did not provide any needed closure for me as a sexual abuse survivor. Not by a long shot. As far as I know, there were no consequences for my cousin for his destructive behavior toward me either. I don't even know if his parents believed my parents about what he had done to me.

Also, my mom and dad didn't talk to me about how this horrible ordeal had impacted me, and they certainly didn't send me of to see some child psychologist to help me. They didn't provide any assurance that my cousin wasn't going to kill me, as he had vowed to do if I ever told on him. I would continue to carry that threat, that fear that felt like it was soul deep, for years.

I was left with the understanding that I should just go on with my life. Forget about what happened. Just be a kid again. But when you have been sexually abused as a boy, it's not that simple.

## The Sibling I Always Wanted

One thing that had not changed for me after that summer of horror and pain was my desire to have someone in our home that I could play with. Like most kids who grow up as an only child in a family, I had always wanted a sibling. Coincidentally or not, after my experience with my cousin I think my parents became much more interested in the idea too.

Since my mom was no longer able to conceive children, they looked into adoption. When they told me that they were considering adopting a girl, I wasn't all that excited at first. I had been envisioning a brother. You know, somebody who would play G.I. Joe with me. Then I remembered all those torturous days and weeks with Jimmy and I thought: *Well, at least girls are not aggressive like boys are.*

My parents even brought Sarah, the girl under consideration for adoption, home to meet me. When that went well, they gave the green light to the adoption process. To celebrate the impending arrival of a sister, they took me out to dinner at The Red Lion, which at the time was one of the fanciest restaurants in the Portland area. I don't remember what I ate for my meal, but I vividly recall the dessert cart they rolled out afterward. I had developed a major sweet tooth by then—I could devour an entire can of frosting in one sitting, and I would drink chocolate syrup straight out of the bottle. Chocolate and cherries were two of my favorite treats, and my parents let me pick one offering of each of the cart. It was a big night!

Sarah, who was around my age give or take a few months, arrived at our home with nothing but a small bag of clothes and one Raggedy Ann doll. She had so few things to wear that my parents immediately took her out to buy her some new clothes. Because she was a girl, my parents did not arrange for her to sleep in the second bed in my room. They converted a small downstairs space into a private room for her.

I was confident that I could get along well with my new sister because I was friends with other girls from our neighborhood. Sarah moved in on a Tuesday, and for the first few days we were friendly toward each other. A good start.

Then came the weekend. On Saturday mornings, I always looked forward to watching my favorite TV show, *Scooby-Doo*. I loved following that lovable Great Dane Scooby as he helped Fred, Daphne, Velma and Shaggy solve all those mysteries. I was lying there under my blanket in bed, still in my PJs, peacefully eating my peanut butter out of the jar with a spoon between sips of milk, when Sarah opened the door to my bedroom and walked in.

"It's *Scooby-Doo*," I said.

"Uh-huh," she said with a nod. Then she proceeded to climb under the blanket with me. While I tried to focus all my attention on the TV, my new sister started to touch me. *Down there!*

"This is what boys in my foster homes would do to me," she said. "It's okay, right?"

I wanted to speak, I really did, but I found myself unable to open my mouth. The words were only brewing inside of me:

*No, no, there's no way this is happening, not again! And she's not just here for the summer, she's . . . permanent.*

I can't tell you how long the touching lasted that first time, or how far it went. I don't remember all the details, only that this was nothing like that time or two I would play "Doctor" with a few of the neighborhood girls when we might have taken a couple of steps in the "you show me yours, I'll show you mine" game but never did any touching. I do remember what Sarah said to me just before she lifted the blanket and climbed out of my bed.

"Don't tell Mom and Dad," she said. "If you do, they'll send me right back, and it will be *your* fault!"

**Scripture:**

**Psalm 35:22, 23 NIV**

*Lord, you have seen this; do not be silent.*

*Do not be far from me, Lord.*

*Awake, and rise to my defense!*

## It Won't Happen Again

Alone in my room, feeling degraded and humiliated, I thought about what I was going to do. I believed that Sarah was right, that if I told my parents they would take her away. If that happened, I would lose the one thing I had really been waiting forever to happen in my life—having a sibling. It was true that what she did was wrong, and that some of those same dirty, creepy feelings I had experienced with my cousin were stirring inside me again. I was shocked, scared, feeling violated. But I also convinced myself that this was different.

"It was just this one time," I said to myself. "I'm sure it won't happen again. She's my sister."

For a few days, that proved to be true. But less than a week later, when I was down in the basement playing with my favorite worn out Teddy bear, my sister approached me again.

"So, what you doing down here?" she asked in a way that felt manipulative and ingenuine from that start.

This time she showed me another side of her behavior, a way of acting that I now understand must have been taught to her, probably in one of her foster homes. Over the next hour or two, with my parents out running errands, Sarah became physically abusive. She displayed her full arsenal of aggressive behavior, which included those arm burns that I remembered from my cousin as well as punching me, pulling my hair and slapping me in the face. And in the midst of it all, there was more touching. Sexual touching. Scary touching.

I was angry as well as hurt and scared, but not once did I try to hit her back or make her stop. Now, I can imagine what you might be thinking: *Wait, Matt. This is a girl! Just beat the crap out of her. Show her you're not going to take any of this bull. Let her know who's boss!*

All I can tell you is that I couldn't, just couldn't. In my brain I kept hearing the words of my father, drilled into me over and over from the time I could first understand him.

"You never hit a girl," he said. "Never. Don't matter what any girl does to you, you just don't hit girls. If you ever do, you will pay the consequences with me."

I had no doubt that he meant it, and I knew him well enough to understand that his "consequences" would hurt much worse than anything my new sister could dish out to me.

> **Understanding Trauma Reminder: Echoes of the messages we received about being a man can make it harder to face the reality of being abused and to ask for help.**

Looking at that experience from my adult understanding today, after years of awareness and healing, I see another factor at play in holding me back. I was still reeling from the emotional and psychological damage delivered over the course of twelve weeks by my older cousin. I fell back into a state of helplessness, along with total confusion. *Why is this all happening to me again? Is everyone out there doing things like this all the time? Or, if it's just me, I must be defective—there must be something inherently wrong with me!*

I wound up in the same abusive position. I was paralyzed in my inaction. And at the same time, somewhere inside a voice was telling me, "You're supposed to be strong, not weak. You should find a way to stop this from happening." Tose words just added a layer of shame on top of the pain and terror. And the other voices, both my dad's warning never to hit a girl and my sister's threats, drowned out any voice that might have pushed me into action.

I have no doubt that had I not been subjected to sexual, physical and verbal abuse with my cousin, I would have reacted differently when my sister began to torment and abuse me. I probably would have told her, "No!" I would have gone to my parents, with an understanding that if my sister's behavior did make them send her back to foster care, that would have been in the best interests of everyone—especially me.

> **Insight for Loved Ones: Be careful not to shame him for winding up in a series of bad relationships by saying something like his "people-picker" is broken. Understand that his "trauma filter" may be doing the choosing for him.**

As it turned out, those two incidents were the only occurrences of that kind of treatment from my sister during the entire first summer she lived with us. That. That renewed my hope that this was not something that would happen on a regular basis. I tried my best to go on with my life.

## Years of Torment

But then, when fourth grade began, my sister purposely scratched me hard enough to leave deep marks on my face on the eve of our class pictures. She was delivering a stronger message: "I am in charge here, and you can never get too comfortable around me."

Sure enough, her physical and sexual aggressiveness became more of a regular thing. And, as I learned at school, she could be just as mean around other kids. She was routinely beating up not only the other girls but also the boys in her class. She even took on and whupped boys who were two or three years older than her.

At home, my sister's mean streak extended to torturing our cat. She would pick up that poor cat, shove it into a small plastic container, close the lid, spray it with water and roll it down the hill. I was horrified. When she told me that she wanted me to do the same thing to my cat, I objected. She looked at me hard and said, "If you don't, I'll just tell Mom and Dad that you are the one who's been doing this to the cat all this time. They'll believe me, not you. You'll be in big trouble."

I agreed to take on the cat torture, and I admit that I did it more than once. Then something kicked in, that same urge to protect that I'd felt toward my friends when my cousin tried to lure them into his circle of abuse. I had to protect my cat! From then on, I would hide the cat when my sister wanted to play her little game, or I would pretend to call it when I was really doing something else. Te cat abuse ceased. I had drawn another line in the sand.

Although I don't think my parents knew what my sister was doing to me, they were certainly hearing about her behavior at school. Maybe they were wondering what they had gotten themselves into by adopting her. It probably wasn't a coincidence that they set out to move our family out of the rougher northeast Portland area where we lived into a home out in a quieter, more rural area in Washington. But if they believed that this move would stop my sister's violent behavior, they were wrong. They hadn't figured on the reception that she and I would receive at a school that had never seen black kids. When the other students tried to pick on my sister or call her racially-charged names, they paid the price through her fury.

By that point, my sister was becoming bolder and more aggressive with me. Her sexual acts, laced with physical abuse, became weekly and, at some point, almost daily. Tis pattern didn't just last for a week, or a month, or even one year. It went on and on for three painful, sickening years. In my confused kid's mind, it reached the point where if for some reason she did *not* approach me to initiate sexual behavior on any particular day, I thought there must be something wrong!

"They'll Blame You!"

My sister also ramped up her threats to keep me in line. Her attempts to intimidate me, warning me that if I told my parents they would send her back, were losing their clout. The reality was that my parents were probably building up lots of potential reasons to reverse the adoption. So, she added a twist.

"If you tell them what we've been doing, they'll blame *you*. You're the boy," she argued. "They'll think you are *really* dirty, and they won't love you anymore."

Tose words shot right to my heart and soul. *She's right! Anyone who finds out what has been happening with me and my sister will think I'm dirty. They won't love me. They won't want to have anything to do with me.*

I felt devalued and hopeless. Still, something inside me, something on a very basic level, must have been looking out for my wellbeing. I knew that my dad had already showed Sarah, more than once, that even girls would face "consequences" for bad behavior. I had seen her challenge my dad, and you don't challenge my dad. There were definitely some whippings going on.

I also had noticed that when my sister would get into trouble with my parents, she would run of into the woods and try to hide for a while, hoping that my parents' frustration and anger would turn into worry and concern so she'd avoid punishment. After one round of my sister punching, grabbing and poking me, I happened to blurt out, "Dad, Sarah's been hitting me." Sure enough, she ran into the woods.

This time, instead of being gone for a half-hour or so, she stayed out all night. The next morning, my dad made a phone call. I was close enough to overhear part of what he was saying. The basic message sounded something like, "We've tried everything we know how to do and nothing is working. We can't help her and give her what she needs. You've got to take her away."

And just like that, my sister really was "going back." The day she left was an emotional roller-coaster for me. I truly and deeply cried, while at the same time I felt instantly safer. And safe was something that I had not felt for years. Mixed with that feeling was a sense of guilt that I was the cause of her leaving, while at the same time I felt proud that maybe I was the reason why she was leaving, like my voice was finally being heard. Everything that had been happening to me over the course of those three painfully long years was over.

**Scripture:**

**Psalm 71:20 NLT**

*You have let me sink down deep in desperate problems. But you will bring me back to life again, up from the depths of the earth.*

**Biblical Insight:**

**A biblical example of a man suffering from sexual abuse**

Unfortunately, sexual abuse has happened against innocent victims since the beginning of time. In Genesis 39, we have the story of Joseph. God was with Joseph, yet he experienced the negative consequences of a woman's sexual assault.

**Story:**

**Genesis 39:6-22 MSG**

*Joseph was a strikingly handsome man. As time went on, his master's wife became infatuated with Joseph and one day said, "Sleep with me."*

*He wouldn't do it. He said to his master's wife, "Look, with me here, my master doesn't give a second thought to anything that goes on here—he's put me in charge of everything he owns. He treats me as an equal. The only thing he hasn't turned over to me is you. You're his wife, after all! How could I violate his trust and sin against God?"*

*She pestered him day after day after day, but he stood his ground. He refused to go to bed with her.*

*On one of these days he came to the house to do his work and none of the household servants happened to be there. She grabbed him by his cloak, saying, "Sleep with me!" He left his coat in her hand and ran out of the house. When she realized that he had left his coat in her hand and ran outside, she called to her house servants: "Look—this Hebrew shows up and before you know it he's trying to seduce us. He tried to make love to me but I yelled as loud as I could. With all my yelling and screaming, he left his coat beside me here and ran outside."*

*She kept his coat right there until his master came home. She told him the same story. She said, "The Hebrew slave, the one you brought to us, came after me and tried to use me for his plaything. When I yelled and screamed, he left his coat with me and ran outside."*

*When his master heard his wife's story, telling him, "These are the things your slave did to me," he was furious. Joseph's master took him and threw him into the jail where the king's prisoners were locked up. But there in jail God was still with Joseph...*

**Biblical Insight:**

**God is with you**

Rest assured that when you were in throes of your abuse, God was still with you.

## Abuse Comes in All Forms

For the second time in my young life, I had endured a long reign of sexual and physical abuse. I took on more scars, suffering additional physical, emotional and psychological damage that would show up in my life in more ways than I could ever imagine. Tis double-dose of sexual trauma would almost destroy my childhood and mess up a whole lot of my early adulthood too.

But I survived. And, many years down the road, I did reach the point in my life where I was able to find the strength and courage to look back at what had happened, and what it had done to me. I was finally able to address the wounds and heal from them. For that, I am eternally grateful.

Now, I realize that some of you reading about my experience with my sister may still be shaking your head and wondering: *Was that really sexual abuse?* After all, Sarah was a girl. And she wasn't seven or eight years older than me; she was about the same age. Well, here's what I have learned about all this:

Abuse comes in all forms, shapes and pictures of who the abuser is. Despite another myth that says that any male, no matter his age or life situation, is "lucky" if any female acts in a sexually aggressive manner toward him, the reality is that males really can and do experience sexual abuse by females. Mother-son incest happens. Female teachers act sexually inappropriately toward young male students. An older sister, the sister of a friend, a female neighbor, an aunt, a babysitter— no matter who the female may be, or what age she is, if she approaches a boy sexually with force or exploits her power, that boy will suffer pain, shame and confusion. Some experts say that almost twenty-five percent of boys who are sexually abused are abused by females.

**Insight for Loved Ones: If a male in your life discloses, even partially, that he has experienced physical or emotional harm from someone, don't discount what he says just because you believe he's physically stronger than that person.**

Boys suffering sexual abuse by females happens, and it happens a lot. In my case, some psychologists might argue that it can't really be "abuse" unless the abuser is many years older than the "victim." To that, I come back to something else I learned about trauma: It's not what happened itself that traumatizes us, it's how we experience the event or series of events.

I know that what I experienced, for me, was abuse. It was trauma. That belief has been a foundation of my healing process.

I don't mention all this to defend myself. No criticism or doubt that I could ever receive for telling this story of my sister's abuse would hurt anything like what she actually did to me for three years. I share my story, and what I made of it, because I know that someone out there reading this book may also have experienced abuse that does not seem to match what typical books about the subject describe.

If you are that person, I don't want you to hold back from getting help out of fear that you won't be believed, that you won't be accepted, that you'll be ridiculed or blamed. If you experienced something that happened as abuse, it was abuse. It's real to you. And you can find the help you need, the support and encouragement that will enable you to address your wounds and claim a healthier life.

I hope you do it soon.

**Scripture:**

**John 16:33 MSG**

*"In this godless world you will continue to experience difficulties. But take heart! I've conquered the world."*

Before moving on, just a quick note about adoption in general. My parents really did adopt Sarah, which means legally she became my sister and their daughter.

The truth is that adoptive families cannot just "unadopt" a child and send them back. Legally, the adopted child becomes part of the family. If parents ever want to change that, they have to disown the child, and that process is no different for adopted kids versus biological kids. There is no secret rip cord.

I mention this just to make sure it doesn't somehow further affirm a deep-seated fear held by someone who is adopted. That type of fear can keep them from ever fully integrating into their adoptive family, and from feeling safely a part of that family.

**Prayer:**

Father,

The world is godless and we all go through many trials and troubles living on this earth. Help me to take heart. You will not override someone else's will, including my own. But You will cause all things to work together for my good. I thank You for it. In Jesus' name,

Amen.

# 4

## MEN EXPERIENCE PHYSICAL TRAUMA

*"It is not the bruises of the body that hurt. It is the wounds of the heart and the scars on the mind."*

- *Aisha Mirza,* writer, DJ and crisis counselor

We don't often hear stories about men who were sexually abused while they were growing up. The shame runs so deep that most men don't share what happened to them with other people in their lives, even if they do acknowledge being sexually abused to themselves. They tend to stay private about it. A rare exception was a 2010 episode of *Oprah* in which 200 men who had survived sexual abuse stood together in public, with featured expert Dr. Howard Fradkin, as a statement that males really are sexually abused.

We tend to hear much more often about boys and men who have been abused physically. That's probably because people are much more willing to accept the reality that men do experience physical trauma.

Still, the male code we talked about in Chapter 1 leads many survivors of physical abuse to deny or minimize the real damage done. You sometimes hear comments like, "Yeah, his dad beat the crap out of him, but I think it just made him tougher." Or, "He got hit until he finally stood up for himself and hit back." Or, "Maybe it was just spanking that got out of hand a few times." Or, "No boy ever gets through his school years without getting picked on by at least one other kid."

Comments like those significantly discount, minimize and under estimate the pain boys and men suffer from physical abuse. Physical abuse causes trauma, and males, no matter how strong or invulnerable they may appear on the outside, are seldom able to escape the damage left behind. That trauma lasts a lot longer than the sting from the blows they absorb.

Let's consider some of the life situations where males may suffer physical trauma. Maybe you have experienced this kind of trauma in one or more of these scenarios, and you are beginning to recognize that the damage is real, something to be acknowledged and addressed.

## Bullying

In recent years, there's been a lot more attention focused on kids, both boys and girls, who are victims of bullying. Parents and entire school communities are beginning to rise up and demand stricter rules and procedures to help bring bullying out of the shadows. Steps are being taken to protect kids who are being bullied while holding the bullies accountable. This is a good start. Our kids need and deserve much closer scrutiny of this form of abuse and much greater protection from beating, hitting, threatening, taunting and other forms of bullying.

You've got to wonder, though, if the efforts underway so far are moving slower than the spread of bullying out there. Maybe others out there would agree with me that the act of bullying is happening a whole lot more than school administrators or communities realize.

Sometimes the spotlight on bullying only gets turned on because of tragedy, when a victim suffers severe injuries or even commits suicide. The bullied boy or girl sometimes leaves behind a trail of pain and desperation on social media or electronic devices. Sadly, it was too late for the trauma of physical abuse to be addressed for that young person. It's also sad for any boy who was bullied a month ago, a year ago, or, for adult men, maybe ten, twenty or thirty years ago.

Bullying, like sexual abuse and other traumas, leaves deep emotional and psychological scars that remain long after the physical healing of assorted bruises, cuts and scratches. It's the invisible wounds that really do the damage.

**Understanding Trauma Reminder: The damage from physical abuse doesn't stop when the physical wounds heal.**

If you carry any memories of being bullied, find someone to talk to about it. Share your secret with a professional trained to assist men in understanding trauma who can help you do what it takes to begin the healing process, or find a support group or other communities of support led by male trauma survivors—they exist all over the country. It doesn't matter whether or not the bullying you suffered included physical acts of hitting or beating. Taunts, ridiculing and criticizing go in just as deep.

Both of my teenage sons have encountered some form of bullying from kids at school. My oldest son was subjected to mean and ruthless comments as he struggled with a degree of autism. The school didn't do a whole lot about it. Fortunately, he had parents who could comfort and support him in getting the help he needed. My younger son went through a period when a boy he knew was stirring up harsh lies about him, lies that kept the other kids from wanting to play with him. Again, my wife and I took steps to intervene, but it pained us to see what our son was being subjected to.

Far too often, however, bullying is not uncovered while it's happening or in the immediate aftermath. That's because bullies combine their aggressive physical acts with forceful threats and intimidation. "Don't tell or I'll really hurt you!" they hiss. Or they'll insist that if their victim ever has the nerve to reveal that he was beaten up and tormented, other boys will call him weak or a sissy. It's a sad reality that sometimes boys wind up hating or ostracizing not the abuser but the "weaker" boy who was abused.

Tose threats that perpetrators deliver often work. Remember the power of threats from my story of the two people who sexually abused me as a boy? In my situation, I was not only verbally threatened by my abusers, I also suffered physical abuse that was delivered along with acts of sexual abuse. I was routinely hit, punched, grabbed, scratched, whacked with wet towels and dealt painful burns on my arms.

Like the bully on the school playground, these perpetrators not only inflicted physical trauma on me, they also knew the right buttons to push with their threats and intimidation. Like me, boys who are bullied often suffer more damaging blows from those threats and the degrading comments about who they are than they do from the physical blows themselves.

If you have ever been bullied, you probably share this experience. Do you remember the words that cut through your heart and soul when the person or people that were bullying you threatened you with greater harm if you told on them? Maybe it's time to talk about that now, and get help for your emotional wounds.

**Biblical Insight:**

**A biblical example of how a bully operates, and how we should respond**

**Scripture:**

**Leviticus 19:16-18 TLB**

*"Don't gossip. Don't falsely accuse your neighbor of some crime, for I am Jehovah.*

*"Don't hate your brother. Rebuke anyone who sins; don't let him get away with it, or you will be equally guilty. Don't seek vengeance. Don't bear a grudge; but love your neighbor as yourself, for I am Jehovah."*

## Beatings and Humiliation at Home

Millions of boys grow up with the deep wounds inflicted by those who beat them, struck them, tortured or tormented them. It may have been their father or stepfather, but it could have been a grandfather, an uncle, an older brother, a friend of the family, another trusted male, or a stranger encountered while in a vulnerable situation. The beatings also may have been administered by a female. I've heard many stories over the years from men that were physically abused in the name of parental punishment by their moms.

The physical trauma might have been inflicted over a long period of time, or it may have been short-term or a one-time occurrence. Either way, the boy who was physically abused suffers pain on many levels.

Let's be clear here. We're not talking about being spanked, which may have been relatively common when you were growing up. I got spanked by my dad sometimes. Some people today may argue otherwise, but I think there's a big difference between getting spanked and being physically abused. I mean, I know my dad was not trying to kill me. His intent was not to leave me crying in pain and agony but to do what he believed he needed to do, just enough to communicate a message about my bad behavior. Ten he stopped.

Perpetrators of physical abuse are driven by a different intention. For some twisted reason, which may be rooted in their own experience of suffering physical trauma, they want to inflict pain and harm. They aim to assert dominance and control. They seek to humiliate and degrade. They're not just *beating* you; they want to *destroy* you with psychological and emotional damage.

For those of us as men who stuff our feelings about being physically abused, that damage sticks to us like fly paper. It can trigger not only intense and recurring anger but also periods of fear, shame or just deep sadness.

Like other traumas, physical abuse also can trigger addictive behavior when we try to numb ourselves to the pain. Or it limits us in our work, or in our intimate relationships. It keeps us in shackles.

Healing from physical abuse helps us break free from those shackles and brings back an authentic sense of power and control over our lives. That is the choice that's always available for any man who suffered physical trauma at any period of his life.

## Biblical Insight:

## A biblical example of a man who suffered gross injustice

Joseph was bullied at the hands of his brothers. He reported their evil behavior to the right authorities, and that is how he ended up in Egypt. They hated him so much, they plotted on how to kill him and get away with it. Later in life, Joseph broke free from the shackles of physical and emotional abuse and became the second in command, only lower than the pharaoh of Egypt! God was with Joseph despite all the abuse he went through. And God was able to save not only Joseph, but his entire clan because Joseph was willing to be unbound from the shackles of trauma!

## Story:

## Genesis 37 MSG

*The story continues with Joseph, seventeen years old at the time, helping out his brothers in herding the flocks. These were his half-brothers actually, the sons of his father's wives Bilhah and Zilpah. And Joseph brought his father bad reports on them.*

*Israel loved Joseph more than any of his other sons because he was the child of his old age. And he made him an elaborately embroidered coat. When his brothers realized that their father loved him more than them, they grew to hate him—they wouldn't even speak to him.*

*Joseph had a dream. When he told it to his brothers, they hated him even more. He said, "Listen to this dream I had. We were all out in the field gathering bundles of wheat. All of a sudden my bundle stood straight up and your bundles circled around it and bowed down to mine."*

*His brothers said, "So! You're going to rule us? You're going to boss us around?" And they hated him more than ever because of his dreams and the way he talked.*

*He had another dream and told this one also to his brothers: "I dreamed another dream—the sun and moon and eleven stars bowed down to me!"*

*When he told it to his father and brothers, his father reprimanded him: "What's with all this dreaming? Am I and your mother and your brothers all supposed to bow down to you?" Now his brothers were really jealous; but his father brooded over the whole business.*

*His brothers had gone off to Shechem where they were pasturing their father's flocks. Israel said to Joseph, "Your brothers are with flocks in Shechem. Come, I want to send you to them."*

*Joseph said, "I'm ready."*

*He said, "Go and see how your brothers and the flocks are doing and bring me back a report." He sent him off from the valley of Hebron to Shechem.*

*A man met him as he was wandering through the fields and asked him, "What are you looking for?"*

*"I'm trying to find my brothers. Do you have any idea where they are grazing their flocks?"*

*The man said, "They've left here, but I overheard them say, 'Let's go to Dothan.'" So Joseph took off, tracked his brothers down, and found them in Dothan.*

*They spotted him off in the distance. By the time he got to them they had cooked up a plot to kill him. The brothers were saying, "Here comes that dreamer. Let's kill him and throw him into one of these old cisterns; we can say that a vicious animal ate him up. We'll see what his dreams amount to."*

*Reuben heard the brothers talking and intervened to save him, "We're not going to kill him. No murder. Go ahead and throw him in this cistern out here in the wild, but don't hurt him." Reuben planned to go back later and get him out and take him back to his father.*

*When Joseph reached his brothers, they ripped off the fancy coat he was wearing, grabbed him, and threw him into a cistern. The cistern was dry; there wasn't any water in it.*

*Then they sat down to eat their supper. Looking up, they saw a caravan of Ishmaelites on their way from Gilead, their camels loaded with spices, ointments, and perfumes to sell in Egypt. Judah said, "Brothers, what are we going to get out of killing our brother and concealing the evidence? Let's sell him to the Ishmaelites, but let's not kill him—he is, after all, our brother, our own flesh and blood." His brothers agreed.*

*By that time the Midianite traders were passing by. His brothers pulled Joseph out of the cistern and sold him for twenty pieces of silver to the Ishmaelites who took Joseph with them down to Egypt.*

*Later Reuben came back and went to the cistern—no Joseph! He ripped his clothes in despair. Beside himself, he went to his brothers. "The boy's gone! What am I going to do!"*

*They took Joseph's coat, butchered a goat, and dipped the coat in the blood. They took the fancy coat back to their father and said, "We found this. Look it over—do you think this is your son's coat?"*

*He recognized it at once. "My son's coat—a wild animal has eaten him. Joseph torn limb from limb!"*

*Jacob tore his clothes in grief, dressed in rough burlap, and mourned his son a long, long time. His sons and daughters tried to comfort him but he refused their comfort. "I'll go to the grave mourning my son." Oh, how his father wept for him.*

## When We Can't Protect Her

Shame gets added to the picture of physical trauma for survivors who can't shake the belief that they should have been able to protect themselves. Part of being a "strong" male means being able to stick up for yourself and stand up to those who may try to harm you, right? Well, for any man who was physically abused as a child, it's a good bet that the person dishing out the abuse was older, or much bigger or stronger physically. But sometimes they're not stronger than you, or they aren't older than you, or they're female. Regardless, it is their intent, which is all about wielding an intense desire to inflict harm. So just how reasonable and realistic is it for anyone to expect a boy to stop his perpetrator? It's not. Most of the time, the best a boy can do when dealing with a prolonged period of physical abuse is to survive. Just get through the experience.

> **Understanding Trauma Reminder: It never helps to beat yourself up for getting beaten up.**

I have known many men who were beaten as boys or adolescents. I also hear stories from men about their father, step-father or mom's boyfriend who didn't beat them, at least not on a regular basis, but did routinely beat their mother. This is another form of trauma for us as males, and it can be just as devastating as suffering the physical abuse ourselves.

First, it hurts to witness your mother being subjected to pain and harm, no matter how well (or not so well) she loved, cared for and nurtured you. It's like you're experiencing the blows right along with her. When you go on with your life, you may carry the same anger, distrust, fear and shame that any boy who was beaten feels.

Tere's another part of this picture that many men tell me about. It's that shame of not being able to protect your mother and your siblings. Some message inside you tells you that even though it's your father, stepfather, your mom's boyfriend or whoever hitting, slapping or punching your mom, and he's bigger than you and has control over you on many levels, you should still be able to rise up and stop him. Never mind that trying to stop him could very well mean putting your life in jeopardy.

Of course, many men who have told me their stories say they did try to step in and protect their moms, not just by shouting at him but by physically taking him on. They decided that they really would "man up" and do what needed to be done. Usually that just left them getting beaten up, too. As a result of them trying to take on the role of protector, they became another punching bag.

The story often goes on to the point where a boy gets old enough and physically strong enough that his demand for this man to stop really does have an effect. Boys who have that experience feel grateful that they could save their moms from more abuse, but the damage from the past has still been done.

Sometimes boys living in a household where physical abuse is happening spend most of their time figuring out how soon they can get out. Whether they go off to college or join the military as soon as they turn eighteen, or get a job and move out of the house as early as possible, they feel a big sense of relief at escaping the scene of the trauma. Yet they may come away with guilt for leaving their mother or any younger siblings behind at home, where those loved ones could have continued to take on more rounds of abuse.

It's often a no-win situation: stay and receive the blows or get out and wind up worrying about other loved ones still absorbing the hits. Men in this experience wind up with layers of trauma: the abuse you suffer yourself, the vicarious trauma of watching the abuser hurting people close to you, the shame of not being able to stop the cycle of abuse, and the feeling of guilt for leaving when others couldn't.

Physical abuse in the home is not always delivered by the hand of a father, stepfather, boyfriend, etc. Tere are also mothers who hit boys. If you're a male who had this happen to you, the trauma can cut even deeper because this is the person who gave you life, a grown-up who's supposed to nurture you. It's your mom!

Boys who survive physical trauma delivered by someone outside their home also come away with a high dose of pain and hurt. Somebody that you trusted or expected to act responsibly did you harm. Sometimes the trauma can be made worse by your decision not to tell anyone what happened, out of fear that no one would believe you or that the abuser would hurt you more.

These are just some of the many ways that males suffer physical trauma. You may have experienced this kind of trauma in a different scenario. Whatever happened to you, no matter how long ago it happened, you can address it now. You can heal. You can build a better life.

**Scripture:**

**Psalm 18:4-6, 16-24 MSG**

*The hangman's noose was tight at my throat;*

*Devil waters rushed over me.*

*Hell's ropes cinched me tight;*

*death traps barred every exit.*

*A hostile world! I call to God,*

*I cry to God to help me.*

*From his palace he hears my call;*

*my cry brings me right into his presence—*

*a private audience!*

*But me he caught—reached all the way*

*from sky to sea; he pulled me out*

*Of that ocean of hate, that enemy chaos,*

*the void in which I was drowning.*

*They hit me when I was down,*

*but God stuck by me.*

*He stood me up on a wide-open field;*

*I stood there saved—surprised to be loved!*

*God made my life complete*

*when I placed all the pieces before him.*

*When I got my act together,*

*He gave me a fresh start.*

*Now I'm alert to God's ways;*

*I don't take God for granted.*

*Every day I review the ways he works;*

*I try not to miss a trick.*

*I feel put back together,*

*and I'm watching my step.*

*God rewrote the text of my life*

*when I opened the book of my heart to his eyes.*

**<u>Prayer:</u>**

Father,

In every hellacious circumstance, I call to You, God, help me! My cry brings me right into Your presence! Pull me out of this ocean of hate, from the chaos of the enemy, the devil! Stick by me, Father, and rescue me! Save me and love me! Make my life complete! Heal the wounds of my broken heart!

Help me to get my act together. Give me a fresh start. Restore my emotions as I carefully watch my steps and walk in Your ways. I give You access to my soul, mind, will, emotions, thoughts, feelings, and purposes. I give You permission to rewrite the text of my life! In Jesus' name,

Amen.

# 5

## MEN EXPERIENCE EMOTIONAL TRAUMA

> *"[Trauma] is the imprints that event has left on your mind and in your sensations...the discomfort you feel and the agitation you feel and the rage and helplessness you feel right now."*
>
> — Bessel van der Kolk, MD
> author, educator, and leading expert on trauma

Any of us who were sexually or physically abused as children had to be strong to survive. We endured moments when we felt helpless and hopeless, degraded and shamed. Moments when we feared that we would not live to see another day. But something inside us, an inner force, kept us going. We may have been damaged, but we were not destroyed. And all along we kept hoping for something or someone to come along in our lives who could make it better, someone who would take the pain that had damaged us and replace it with something good.

For me, that "something" was going to be basketball. The trauma that I had suffered as a child did not take away all my dreams, and the dream that I focused all my time and energy on was to play pro basketball. Sure, the odds were overwhelmingly against me, but try telling that to any kid who sets off to make it onto the NBA stage.

So, despite all the craziness in my life, all the trauma and pain I was carrying that I had not even begun to address, I took to hoops to keep me going. As it turned out, I was naturally gifted at basketball, so devoting most of my free time to dribbling, shooting and trying to put together games with friends to improve my skills just seemed to fit. I excelled on my eighth-grade team that completed an undefeated season, and I shined at every basketball camp I attended. People were beginning to talk about my game. I felt like I was starting to become a somebody.

## A Refuge from the Pain

Looking back at that time today, I can see how basketball was my escape from the pain, my refuge, my safe place where I could somehow try to repair my shattered identity from years of abuse and reclaim some of my lost self-esteem. It was an essential part of my survival.

In my freshman year of high school, I was becoming even more of a somebody. Freshmen were not allowed on the varsity team at that time, but I was the best freshman player in our entire league.

Around this time, my self-esteem rose another notch when I stumbled upon a book about Martin Luther King, Jr. in the library and read it with far more interest than any assigned reading material in class. I came away from reading that book with some sense rising up inside me that one day my life would have some impact on other people. That's a pretty big step for a young abuse survivor!

Then things began to change, and the dream I was clutching soon began to slip away. Yep, I was about to be hit by another one of those trauma buses. This one came in the form of emotional and verbal abuse.

As I mentioned earlier, my parents had moved our family to a rural area well outside of Portland, bringing us to a place where blacks were few in number. I remember hearing about how some kids had come to the high school that I was assigned to dressed in Ku Klux Klan outfits for Halloween. That was scary!!! When my parents concluded that it would not serve my education to stay in that hostile environment, they arranged for me to begin my sophomore year at a much safer school.

That meant I would be playing on a different high school basketball team, which sounded fine to me. That school's summer league team played against the team I was on, and I liked the way those guys carried themselves. It looked like they were having a good time. Then I checked out the school. Brand new facilities, including a new gym. This was going to be great!

The head basketball coach happened to be my science teacher, so I had a chance to get to know him a few months before we even started practice. Sometimes, while his class was taking a test or doing a quiet assignment, he would bring me into his office and start going over some of the plays we would be running. It meant a lot that he was taking an interest in me, when I hadn't even begun playing for this school. I was even more excited for my first season to begin.

I did well enough in practice to earn a starting position on the team as a sophomore, and as the season began, we were clicking. Things were definitely looking up. For me, that dream of playing pro basketball was coming into closer view.

"You're a Nobody!"

My coach continued his private meetings with me in his office, but suddenly his whole tone and demeanor toward me did a 180.

Instead of telling me about what I was doing right, he was now telling me only what he believed I was doing wrong. At first, he limited his criticism to my performance on the court. He wanted me to change things about my game: my shooting, my defense, everything. But soon his verbal assessments extended into what felt like a complete criticism of me as a *person*. He told me my attitude was lousy:

> *"You're not tough enough, Burton." "Burton, you just don't have enough heart."*

He even told me who I should and should not hang out with at school. He judged some of my personal habits. It went on and on, and after a while my coach's words just got filtered in my brain and spun out as the words from my cousin who abused me. *You're a zero. You're a waste. You're nobody.*

> **Insight for Loved Ones: Even when it may seem socially acceptable for boys to be spoken to harshly by coaches or teachers, understand that sometimes those words, actions or demands are abusive and can shred his self-esteem. Stand up and protect him!**

I did my best to make the adjustments that my coach wanted me to make on the court, but I felt so afraid that I was just going to hear more criticism from him, I wound up struggling with things that I used to do well. Despite the thousands of hours that I had spent practicing since I was a young kid, and despite having a vertical reach as high as some pro players, I started to question my ability. And I wanted those voices I was suddenly hearing from this coach, made louder by the echoes from my cousin, to just stop.

My self-esteem began to show signs of distress, not just around the team but all over school. One day my English teacher, Ms. Thompkins, asked me what was wrong. Since she had always shown a sincere interest in me, I explained to her what was going on with my basketball coach.

"I think I'm going to have to quit the team," I said.

"Matt," she said, "basketball is too important to you. You can't quit!"

Ms. Thompkins went on to offer me additional words of encouragement and support. I felt even more strongly that this was someone who really cared about me. Someone who believed in me.

I didn't quit. Inspired by this teacher's personal interest and validation of who I was, and despite the treatment I was receiving from my coach, I began to play better. The team began to win, and newspaper articles starting referring to me as "Super Soph." We advanced to districts and then on to the state tournament in Seat tle. Even though we didn't do as well there, it had been a very successful season. I was the only sophomore to start at state. During the last few weeks of the season, my coach had even begun to back off on his putdowns and criticism. I thought maybe things were going to be all right after all.

I regained my enthusiasm for playing basketball, and as my junior season approached, I was even more excited because, with the seniors from last year's team graduated, I figured I would become the team's anchor. Everything was looking up.

**Biblical Insight:**

Leaders are the role models for their followers, and harsh treatment of others is an abomination to God.

**Scripture:**

**Ephesians 4:29-32 AMP**

*Watch the way you talk. Let nothing foul or dirty come out of your mouth. Say only what helps, each word a gift.*

*Don't grieve God. Don't break his heart. His Holy Spirit, moving and breathing in you, is the most intimate part of your life, making you fit for himself. Don't take such a gift for granted.*

*Make a clean break with all cutting, backbiting, profane talk. Be gentle with one another, sensitive. Forgive one another as quickly and thoroughly as God in Christ forgave you.*

## Burton's Law?

Unfortunately, I hurt my knee while working extra hard in the weight room, and the resulting surgery kept me sidelined for the first few weeks of the new season. During my recovery from my injury, the largest newspaper in our region approached me to do an article about me. It was nice to get the attention, but I felt a little embarrassed when I read the headline: "Burton's Law Rules."

Of course, my coach saw that headline too. Immediately he called the whole team together and in his most authoritative voice he announced, "Let's be very clear here. On this team MY law rules!" As if to demonstrate how seriously he meant that statement, and to remind me and everybody else what my law was worth, he started making me the center of attention in a way that no player would ever want. Whenever he made the team do an extra drill, or he assigned extra running because of something he didn't like on the court, it was always "Burton's fault." When we lost a game, that had to be "Burton's fault" too.

Off the court, his putdowns, criticisms and judgments about who I was and how I lived my life returned to the previous season's levels, and soon surpassed them. I had truly become the coach's whipping boy.

At least I still had summer camps. I was even selected for an all-star team that competed in Sweden, Finland and Denmark before touring Leningrad (now St. Petersburg), Russia. I still remember playing at the Olympic training center in Stockholm, Sweden, as well as our time in Leningrad, not far from the famous Hermitage Museum and Saint Isaac's Cathedral across the street. Participating in such a prestigious trip (and chasing some Scandinavian girls around!) took some of the sting away from the verbal and emotional abuse I faced back on my high school team.

I continued to gain accolades as a basketball player in my state and region. At one point I was encouraged by some of the players from Mercer Island High School to transfer there. That was the school where Quin Snyder played before he went on to excel at Duke and eventually become coach of the Utah Jazz in the NBA. One of the players had even arranged for me to come live with the family of one of the team's players. That was an exciting possibility for me, the idea of being out of the grasp of my high school coach and getting a chance to take my game higher. Unfortunately, my parents vetoed that plan.

For my senior year, it was back to the same emotionally abusive pattern. If I thought things were bad during my junior season, I would soon discover that they would pale in comparison to what was in store for me for my final year. Not only did my coach maintain his verbal assaults on my playing and my character, making fun of me and even my girlfriend, he also pressured my teammates not to vote for me for team captain.

Then, when the games began, he started pulling me out every time I made any kind of "mistake." And he went a step further. He instructed the guards on our team not to pass me the ball.

Although I was hurt even more by this bizarre move, I did not lose my desire to excel. If I wasn't going to get the ball from my teammates passing it to me, I would just have to grab every available rebound. That's how I became the top rebounder, not only on our team but in our region. Still, I was shaken and suffering inside, and at times that showed up on the court in the form of things like air balls on my free throws.

Despite this abusive treatment, I was doing well and so was our team. In fact, we completed the regular season with a perfect 20-0 record. When we entered the district playoffs, we went up against a team that we had just blown out by twenty points. But in this game, the cracks in our team opened up. We played really badly. When our coach called timeout with just a few seconds left in the game, we were behind by one point. We had one more shot to avoid an embarrassing loss that would end our season.

As I listened to our coach begin to explain the strategy for our final play, I was already gearing myself up for getting in position to try to rebound any missed shot that would be taken by whoever he chose to attempt it. Maybe I could save our team with a last-second rebound basket. Then I heard the words. *Pass it to Burton. Give him the ball for our last shot to win the game.*

My head was spinning out of control. The silent monologue in my brain was coming out something like this: "Let me get this straight. You've spent the last two and a half seasons telling me how horrible I am. You've gone out of your way to humiliate me. You've criticized me for everything about my game, my personality, my life. You've pulled me off the court for every little mistake. You've destroyed my self-esteem. And all season long you've been telling our guards not to pass me the ball. Now you're standing there saying, 'Matt, it's time for you to win the game for us so we can move on, get a step closer to states.' No, I don't think so."

When one of my teammates followed our coach's instructions and passed me the ball, I passed it back to one of our talented sophomores. With only one second left on the clock, he had no choice but to take that last shot. It missed, and before I could crash in and fight for the rebound, the buzzer sounded. We lost.

I didn't cry about this shocking upset or the jarring end to our season. The truth was, I wasn't sad at all that my high school basketball career was done. I was incredibly relieved. My long experience of being the recipient of verbal and emotional trauma was, at long last, over.

**Understanding Trauma Reminder: Being verbally and emotionally abused can drain the joy out of your life, filling your mind with doubt, negative self-talk and shame, until it is addressed and healed.**

I was too shell-shocked to even attend the postseason team banquet. My dad went in my place, explaining to my teammates and everyone else that "Matt isn't feeling well." Well, that was one way to put it.

Even then, the trail of verbal and emotional abuse from this basketball coach was not over. I had still hung on to those dreams of going further in my basketball career, and knowing that my coach would not be touting my name to potential college basketball recruiters, I took it upon myself to send letters and video highlights of my game to top-notch programs like Duke, North Carolina and Georgetown. It didn't matter. My coach pulled me aside one last time and emphatically informed me that if any recruiter contacted him with any degree of interest in me, he was going to tell them that I had the worst attitude of any player he had ever coached. They'd be crazy to even consider offering me a scholarship to play college basketball.

And that's how it happened that the only offer I did receive was from Warner Pacific College, a small Christian school in Portland. I accepted their offer, but with additional surgical procedures on my knee, bringing me up to a total of five surgeries in three years, my basketball career soon ended.

**Biblical Insight:**

**God restores and protects His people**

In Isaiah 41, Isaiah speaks to the Jews who were ruthlessly conquered by Babylon and exiled. Now, their 70-year captivity was coming to a close, and the nation of Israel lay in ruins.

God assures His covenant people that they will be restored. He also warns the surrounding nations that they are about to witness an amazing miracle. Although they were destroyed for their idolatry, God is in the business of total and complete restoration. If He will do it for an entire nation, He will do it for you!

**Scripture:**

**Isaiah 41:14-21 MSG**

*"Do you feel like a lowly worm, Jacob?*
*Don't be afraid.*
*Feel like a fragile insect, Israel?*
*I'll help you.*
*I, God, want to reassure you.*
*The God who buys you back, The Holy of Israel.*
*I'm transforming you from worm to harrow,*
*from insect to iron.*
*As a sharp-toothed harrow you'll smooth out the mountains,*
*turn those tough old hills into loamy soil.*
*You'll open the rough ground to the weather,*
*to the blasts of sun and wind and rain.*
*But you'll be confident and exuberant,*
*expansive in The Holy of Israel!*

*The poor and homeless are desperate for water,*
*their tongues parched and no water to be found.*
*But I'm there to be found, I'm there for them,*
*and I, God of Israel, will not leave them thirsty.*
*I'll open up rivers for them on the barren hills,*
*spout fountains in the valleys.*
*I'll turn the baked-clay badlands into a cool pond,*
*the waterless waste into splashing creeks.*
*I'll plant the red cedar in that treeless wasteland,*
*also acacia, myrtle, and olive.*
*I'll place the cypress in the desert,*
*with plenty of oaks and pines.*
*Everyone will see this. No one can miss it—*
*unavoidable, indisputable evidence*
*That I, God, personally did this.*
*It's created and signed by The Holy of Israel."*

## The Deep Pit of Trauma

Looking back on this whole ordeal, I realize that other people might interpret what happened to me differently. They might argue that this basketball coach just wanted to keep my ego under control. And just as there is the code among males that we must man up to face any kind of adversity and prove our mettle as a male, some people involved in boys' sports might say that sometimes a coach has to beat down a star player in order to build him back up again to a place where he achieves his full potential.

To that I say, give me a break. In my situation, my experience of what was dealt to me was always going to be influenced by the trauma I had already suffered. My self-esteem had been shattered by sexual and physical abuse. If I was going to have any chance to achieve my full potential as an athlete and as a human being, I needed the exact opposite of what I got.

I needed more people like Ms. Thompkins. People who believed in me. People who understood my vulnerability. People who could see that any confidence I was beginning to display could be easily crushed and required constant faith and nurturance to keep intact and, hopefully, grow. People who really, really wanted me to feel good about myself, and to shine for others to see.

> **Insight for Loved Ones: Keep close watch over what all the adults in his life are saying/doing to him, and assess whether it is or is not beneficial for not just his physical health but his emotional health.**

Sometimes boys and young men who survive verbal or emotional trauma are fortunate enough to receive just that kind of caring, supportive treatment somewhere along the way. They are the ones who are truly blessed.

Most of us, however, tend to find that the trauma that is wearing us down just sticks to us like fly paper. Or it just gets worse, with more layers of trauma hooking on to us from new directions, in new shapes and forms. Eventually that trauma starts triggering one or more symptoms of unresolved trauma that we have talked about: addictions, broken relationships, career and financial setbacks, intense anger or deep sadness. Or something worse.

As I will be illustrating in later chapters, it is the weight of those symptoms that more often than not finally leads us to try to fight our way out of the deep pit of trauma. It shoves us toward that place where we finally ask for help.

Then, when we address the pain and trauma, and begin to take active steps toward healing, we make a surprising discovery: the caring, supportive, understanding and generally positive treatment that we had yearned to receive from others while suffering through our trauma is something that we can actually begin to deliver *ourselves.*

There are so many great discoveries that await you when you make the choice to address the pain and suffering that trauma has dumped on you. That's true whether you suffered sexual trauma or physical trauma or if, like my experience that you just witnessed, the trauma that mowed you over came in the form of verbal or emotional abuse.

Maybe, like me, you got that kind of abusive treatment from a coach of a sports team. Or maybe it was a teacher. Or your first serious love relationship partner. Or your boss. Or maybe it was a parent who seemed to know every possible way to demean and degrade you without ever laying a hand on you.

No matter who showered that verbal or emotional abuse on you, and no matter what age or in what environment it occurred, you are not alone. I have a pretty good idea of what that may have felt like to you, and the professional caregivers or supportive peers you reach out to are ready to respond to you in a way that shows that they understand, that they care, that they will commit themselves to helping you heal.

It's never too late to reclaim your self-esteem. It's never too late to dream new dreams.

**Biblical Insight:**

**Paul places expectations on Church leaders**

The Apostle Paul established leaders for the church, and he outlined the qualities of good leadership. Here, he follows Christ's example of leadership and expects those he trained to do the same.

**Story:**

**Acts 20:15-31 MS**
*And so this is good-bye. You're not going to see me again, nor I you, you whom I have gone among for so long proclaiming the news of God's inaugurated kingdom. I've done my best for you, given you my all, held back nothing of God's will for you.*

*Now it's up to you. Be on your toes—both for yourselves and your congregation of sheep. The Holy Spirit has put you in charge of these people—God's people they are—to guard and protect them. God himself thought they were worth dying for.*

*I know that as soon as I'm gone, vicious wolves are going to show up and rip into this flock, men from your very own ranks twisting words so as to seduce disciples into following them instead of Jesus. So stay awake and keep up your guard. Remember those three years I kept at it with you, never letting up, pouring my heart out with you, one after another.*

**<u>Prayer:</u>**

Father,

You will smooth out mountains of trauma in my life and the lives of others. You will turn rough old hills into loamy soil so there can be a wonderful harvest of fruit.

You are turning me into someone who is confident and exuberant. You are improving the quality of my life and expanding my influence. Everyone will see that it is You, Father, who has created me in the image of Your Son, Jesus Christ. I credit all the glory in my life to You! In Jesus' name,

Amen.

## 6

## MEN EXPERIENCE LOSS, REJECTION AND ABANDONMENT

*"Some things can be so horrifying that they metaphorically turn us to stone."*

- Jasmin Lee Cori, *Healing from Trauma*

Remember those myths about men that we debunked in Chapter 1? As a reminder, one of them went like this:

*Men don't really hurt, because they are so strong.*

In the last few chapters, we've been looking at the many ways that men really do experience pain and hurt when they suffer various forms of abuse. Well, here's something else to know about how men get hurt emotionally, psychologically or spiritually: it doesn't always come from getting hit by one of those buses that represent a trauma like physical abuse, sexual abuse or verbal and emotional abuse.

The truth is that pain isn't necessarily dealt to us by a one-time jolting event, or a series of events. Sometimes, the hurt can come in the form of a deep sadness or sorrow delivered by things that happen in our lives that leave us with a major sense of loss. Or rejection. Or abandonment.

Experiences of loss, rejection and abandonment that can cause men real hurt and pain cover a wide territory that would take a whole book to navigate. We're just going to take a quick look at a few of them here.

I'll share a few relevant stories from my own life where they can help illustrate the many shapes of loss, rejection and abandonment, and I'll bring in some experiences from other men I have known and guided toward the healing path. You might recognize yourself in some of these accounts, or you might identify a different experience that you lived through that relates to this kind of trauma.

## Rejected Before I Was Born

Let's start with rejection. As I mentioned earlier, I am half-black and half-white. It so happens that my mom's father and her older brothers were not at all pleased when their tall, blonde Dutch daughter (or sister) revealed that the love of her life was an African American male. Stories I have heard from my family have made it dramatically clear that my dad was totally rejected by my mom's family.

Then I entered the picture. As I tell people, I feel like I was rejected before I was even born. Just as my mom's parents didn't want anything to do with my dad, they didn't want anything to do with me when I came along either. For years and years, I didn't even meet anyone from my mom's family. As a child and even as I grew up, I couldn't understand this rejection. I always thought that grandparents were supposed to love and embrace their grandkids. It seemed crazy to me that I was being rejected on the basis of race.

I didn't talk about this much as a kid. At least I did have the presence of people from my dad's family—for better or, in the case of my older cousin, for worse. But then I got a more personal taste when I played high school basketball. I would talk to girls at school, we'd hit it off, and I'd ask them out. They were usually excited and said "sure," but one after another would call me or tell me in class a day or two later that they couldn't go out with me. Why? The reason was always the same: their parents didn't want their daughter going out with a black guy. It was incredibly hurtful to have these same men, these same dads, come to watch me play basketball. And it's not the only time I've been rejected or discriminated against just for who I am.

Have you ever felt rejected by someone important in your life? Did you shrug it off at the time as no big deal? Maybe the sting of the rejection impacted you more than you would admit to others, or even to yourself. And maybe it's time for you to begin to lift the lid, let that pain out of the box and get help in processing it.

**Scripture:**

**Isaiah 49:15 MSG**

*Can a mother forget the infant at her breast,*

*walk away from the baby she bore?*

*But even if mothers forget,*

*I'd never forget you—never.*

## The Sting of Abandonment

In my life, my parents at least stayed together and remained part of my life. Millions of guys grow up in homes where one or both parents exit from their lives, either for an important period in their upbringing or forever. When a father or mother leaves not only their marriage but their presence as a caregiver, it can leave a gaping hole for any boy.

This is where we as men can get tricked into that male way of denying or minimizing. We can say, "Yeah, my dad left home when I was five, but that didn't bother me. I mean, I never really knew him anyway and I heard from my mom that I wasn't missing much." Or "It's true that my mom no longer raised me from the time I was very young, but she couldn't help it—she was on drugs." Our words may be true, but they don't tell the complete story. Somewhere inside we still feel that pain and loss that comes when somebody who was supposed to love and care for us left us behind. We got lit up by abandonment.

**Understanding Trauma Reminder:** *The* **hurt from childhood abandonment is like a layer of** *fi*lm **that colors and distorts every part of our lives, as well as our relationships, and it needs to be addressed.**

Many men have shared with me that growing up as the son of a mother or father addicted to alcohol or drugs definitely left a deep imprint on their lives. There are many books about the children of alcoholics written by professionals who describe the fear, anger, loneliness, guilt, embarrassment, distrust of other people, and loss of confidence or direction that those who grew up around alcoholics suffer. Women tend to be more likely to recognize and act upon the impact of that kind of upbringing. Men are more likely to dismiss it, insisting that it wasn't any real influence on them. Yet their lives are still very much impacted.

If your life shows any signs of being messed up or seems consistently off-track, and you know or suspect that one or both of your parents were alcoholics or drug addicts, or were addicted to prescription drugs, pornography, work or food, and they were not just physically absent but emotionally absent too, please be aware that there are 12-Step groups for adult children of alcoholics that can help you. Also, most 12-Step groups have "anon" groups for the loved ones impacted by the addiction: Al-Anon, N-Anon (narcotics), etc., as well as trained counselors to talk to. You owe that to yourself.

**Scripture:**

**Psalm 27:10 MSG**

*My father and mother walked out and left me,*

*but God took me in.*

## The Hole Left by Loss

Many of us experience some kind of significant loss in our lives. The premature death of a parent, grandparent, sibling or other loved one during childhood or as an adult can leave behind a well of sadness. We carry that unresolved and unexpressed sadness into our adult years.

The good news is that with the help of professional caregivers, support groups and many other healing resources, along with a commitment to build awareness, there are ways to effectively grieve and mourn the loss of a loved one. I'll tell you about a surprising round of grief and loss I experienced well into my adult years in a moment.

First, let's talk about the loss that millions of men experience: divorce. We know that half of all marriages end in divorce, so there's a pretty good chance you witnessed divorce growing up. Watching your parents get divorced can be a very traumatic experience for any child, especially when your mom and dad are in open conflict and you suffer from the fallout.

As an adult, if your own marriage ends in divorce, that can bring about sadness and other painful feelings on a number of fronts.

No matter what led to the divorce, you may feel like a failure. Or you lose confidence in your ability to enter into healthy relationships. You may feel lost and alone. You may feel guilt for anything you did that you think caused the divorce.

**Scripture:**

**John 16: 31-33 MSG**

*Jesus answered them, "Do you finally believe? In fact, you're about to make a run for it—saving your own skins and abandoning me. But I'm not abandoned. The Father is with me. I've told you all this so that trusting me, you will be unshakable and assured, deeply at peace. In this godless world you will continue to experience difficulties. But take heart! I've conquered the world."*

## Divorce Court Blues

Going through a divorce also can leave us holding heaps of anger, bitterness or a sense of injustice. The anger usually comes from all those ways we may feel mistreated and misunderstood by our spouse. The injustice often gets doubled-down by what happens to us in the legal system. I got stung there, and I know I am definitely not alone on that one.

Regardless of who is at fault for the brokenness that leads to the end of a marriage, once a couple starts down the legal path around divorce, the power dynamic changes quickly and one-sidedly. It seems as if the family court system is set up to protect women, especially moms. I can still feel the devastation from my divorce, and the pain I felt from what happened to me in court. I busted my butt to try to obtain equal custody of my young daughter, but at the end of the day I was granted what most men are awarded: Wednesdays and every other weekend.

I've talked to dozens of men with similar stories. It seems like it doesn't matter if you have a great job, not much of a job or no job—the kind of decree I got is about what you're going to get as a dad in custody battles. And if you challenge the ruling, you almost always lose. Like it or not, men typically come away from divorce court feeling like they got shafted, that the whole system is skewed toward women.

Did you ever find yourself taking on this unwanted and unwelcome hit? You certainly have a right to feel angry and bitter about that, but here's the thing: carrying anger and bitterness about getting screwed over by divorce, or anything else in life, only hurts ourselves in the long run. At some point, we need to look at those feelings, process them and cross over to the other side of our life.

**Understanding Trauma Reminder: Holding on to bitterness about your divorce can block you from creating what you want in life today for you and your kids.**

That doesn't mean we should pretend that our spouse and the court were right about everything, that things really were fair when we know they weren't. It just means that we need to recognize that at some point we have to take responsibility for dealing with our hurts, and the wounds that we created in others, if we're going to go on and create good things in our life. Resentment doesn't ever help us. I've heard it said many times that holding onto resentment is like drinking poison and expecting the other person to die.

Okay, I admit that it took me a long time to wake up to that reality. In my mind, I could tell anyone who would listen a clear-cut story of all those ways that I believed I was wronged, and for a while there I clung so tightly to my story that it threatened to eat me up. This was a loss that really shattered me.

Fortunately, with the guidance of those who wanted what was best for me, I finally came to see that I had to grieve that loss so that I could move past it. To get there, I had to face a major choice: to remain bitter toward my ex-wife and the family court system that seemed to penalize me just for being a male, or to acknowledge that my ex-wife and I *both* contributed in a negative way to the breakup of our marriage. I made the second choice. I recognized that I needed to take ownership of all the stuff on my side of the street and stop fixating on what was going on over on the other side of the street.

If I had not made that choice, and if I didn't take the time to grieve that loss, I would have just brought all the baggage and wounds that I experienced from that marriage into my next marriage. I decided that was not something I wanted to do. Because I had the strength to make that choice, I have a healthy and satisfying marriage today with my second and final wife Laura.

Our legal system seems to come up with lots of ways to throw fiery balls of pain at men when it comes to our marriages. To give you one example, I'll bring in the story of Bart, a guy who got caught in the legal flames so bad he didn't think he was going to get out.

### The Other Side of Intimate Partner Abuse

I learned about Bart's situation through his dad, a professional colleague of mine. Bart's wife had kicked him out of the house and accused him of physically hitting her. Charged with domestic violence, Bart got hauled off to jail. But from what I understand, Bart was not treated fairly by the court. There was another side to his story, but for far too long, no one seemed willing to listen to that one.

On several different occasions, long before he was arrested, Bart knew that he needed to get help for what was happening with his wife. You see, she was actually physically abusing Bart. He went to the police—twice—but was given no assistance. Why? Because he was a man and women never beat up their men!

> **Insight for Loved Ones: Just from stories of my friends and acquaintances, I have been shocked by how prevalent physical abuse of men by women really is. As a loved one, when you hear about this happening, take it seriously.**

Bart also reached out to a mental health crisis line to get his wife help for her mental health issues. That didn't change things either.

At some point Bart turned to his wife's family for help, and he got a cold response on that front as well. Things got so serious that he wound up taking his wife to the hospital ER to seek medical assistance, and he didn't find satisfaction there.

Eventually, Bart recognized that he had no choice but to file for divorce. That's when his wife made up a story about Bart abusing her. Add to this scenario the fact that she was pregnant at the time she made these allegations, and the police believed her but wouldn't believe Bart. Eventually, he wound up agreeing to criminal charges for something he didn't do in a plea deal to avoid a possible felony charge. He lost his job along the way and, for a period of time, he was even prevented from seeing his son.

Fortunately, Bart wound up in the expert hands of a counselor specializing in intimate partner abuse. Slowly but surely, he's been putting his life back together again. He landed another job, paved the way to establish an active relationship with his son. Now divorced and single for many years, he's planning to marry a woman with whom he has a healthy and stable connection.

Those positive developments would not have happened if Bart had remained bitter and just kept spending all his time and energy battling against the injustice he suffered on the legal battlefield. He had the doors to a better life opened to him because he got help for his emotional pain from a professional who understood him.

**Biblical Insight:**

God expects both marriage partners to be integrous, and He hates abuse. God does not want anyone to remain in an abusive relationship.

**Scripture:**

**Malachi 2:15, 16 MSG**

*God, not you, made marriage. His Spirit inhabits even the smallest details of marriage. And what does he want from marriage? Children of God, that's what.*

*So guard the spirit of marriage within you. Don't cheat on your spouse. "I hate divorce," says the God of Israel. God-of-the-Angel-Armies says, "I hate the violent dismembering of the 'one flesh' of marriage." So watch yourselves. Don't let your guard down.*

## Losing Our Jobs

As men, we also frequently suffer loss related to our jobs or careers. That can happen for many reasons. Whether you're the owner of your own business that you built up from nothing, or you're toiling away at some routine work-a-day job, when the plug gets pulled, it can feel like part of you got sucked right down the drain too. It often seems that as men, we are defined by our jobs. When we lose our job, we lose a big part of our identity.

**Insight for Loved Ones: You also may feel shell-shocked by the loss of his job or business, not just financially but emotionally. Find a way to process and resolve what you're experiencing individually and as a family.**

As men, we're not inclined to stop for a moment and say, "Wait, what just happened here? Who can I talk to so I can get help for this feeling of getting hit by a ton of bricks?" Instead, we just say, "Where can I find another job (or a new business to build) and how fast can I do it?" Then we fail to acknowledge that we're drinking a lot more. Or we're constantly getting angry with our wives, our kids and almost everyone else we deal with. We don't see that the unresolved feelings from our loss have taken over our lives.

**Biblical Insight:**

God hates unfair work practices. He hates every type of abuse.

**Scripture:**

**Jeremiah 22:13-17 MSG**

*"Doom to him who builds palaces but bullies people,*

*who makes a fine house but destroys lives,*

*Who cheats his workers*

*and won't pay them for their work,*
*Who says, 'I'll build me an elaborate mansion*
*with spacious rooms and fancy windows.*
*I'll bring in rare and expensive woods*
*and the latest in interior decor.'*
*So, that makes you a king—*
*living in a fancy palace?*
*Your father got along just fine, didn't he?*
*He did what was right and treated people fairly,*
*And things went well with him.*
*He stuck up for the down-and-out,*
*And things went well for Judah.*
*Isn't this what it means to know me?"*
*God's Decree!*
*"But you're blind and brainless.*
*All you think about is yourself,*
*Taking advantage of the weak,*
*bulldozing your way, bullying victims."*

## Losing a Loved One

The biggest loss that many of us will ever suffer comes when a loved one dies. Most of us have had someone close to us pass away, whether it was when we were just a young kid or during our adult life. When the death is premature or unexpected, it can really be a tough blow. In our sadness and grief, we face the challenge of dealing with the void. And then, as men, we confront the voices that tell us we've got to be strong, to be there for everybody else.

While I was in the sauna several weeks ago, I started talking to a guy who worked out at our local club the same time I did. I asked him how he was doing, and he mentioned that he had lost his wife a couple of weeks earlier. As I do whenever some guy tells me about some trauma he has been hit with, I offered a listening ear. I acknowledged the pain he must have been feeling and gave him space to talk about anything he wanted to bring up.

Well, part of what he went on to talk about was that his daughter was really struggling with the loss of her mom, and his grandson couldn't even talk about it. He said that no matter how he was doing, he felt he had to be there for them. I nodded my head. Then I suggested that sometimes, even as guys, we have to just let ourselves break down. And get some help when we do. I also suggested that he join a grief support group. I explained that I had gone to a grief group through our local hospital for six months a few years earlier to process grief of my own and that it had really helped me.

**Scripture:**

**Psalm 116:15 NIV**

***Precious in the sight of the Lord is the death of his faithful servants.***

## The Tragedy of Suicide

The loss that comes in the form of suicide totally rocks the world of all the loved ones of the deceased. Suicide leaves behind what feels like a bottomless pit of grief, and a long trail of questions that just don't seem to have any answers.

Gary has been wrestling with those questions and the deep grief from losing his son Sam to suicide five years ago. I heard his story after I met him at one of my "Unbound Man" talks around helping men heal from trauma.

Sam was a student at a university in the Midwest when Gary and his family back home in Oregon heard the shocking and demoralizing news about their son. "Everyone who knew him would say he was the last person on earth you would expect this to happen to. It was not even on the radar," Gary recalled.

For years after the tragedy, Gary would go off by himself every morning when he woke up and every night before he went to bed to try to process what happened, to attempt to understand something that nobody can really understand. He tossed around the same questions: Why did it happen? How did we miss the signs? Was there something we as parents could have done?

Gary and his wife knew that Sam was a perfectionist, a boy self-driven to excel academically. As a twelve-year-old, he mastered a calculus training kit five minutes after his dad had given it to him. That perfectionism stuck with him all through high school and on into college. They also heard that there had been a break-up with a girlfriend not long before the tragedy.

As Gary and his family continued to do their best to wade through the well-known stages of grief—denial, anger, bargaining, depression, acceptance—they also gained a deeper understanding of the many contributing factors related to suicide. They learned about a dynamic of many teens and young adults exhibiting signs of what's often called "smiling depression," where the individual masks his or her pain and hopelessness from those around them. They were taught about how the stigma of mental illness and certain forms of trauma often prevent young people like Sam from reaching out for help. That barrier can lead struggling individuals toward either "acting out" by hurting others or "acting in" by hurting themselves. And as a Christian family, they gained first-hand experience of the stigma often associated with a loved one taking their own life.

Beyond all these new teachings, Gary and his family simply hurt. Deeply. Sam's two younger sisters adored him for his kind, gentle personality. As a brother, he displayed limitless patience and a creative spark that would show up in simple activities like organizing a three-sibling cupcake baking competition, where no one was allowed to use a recipe. Even outside the family, Sam would put the needs of others ahead of his own. While working to assist the homeless in his community, he volunteered to live briefly as a homeless person himself, just so he could better understand the experience.

But just remembering the details of your loved one's life doesn't fill in the blanks after suicide. As Gary's head kept spinning with all the whys, he decided that he had a choice of how to deal with his devastating loss: he could climb under a rock and try somehow to forget about it all, or he could get active and do something to help other people. He made that second choice. He and his wife got involved with Active Minds, a national suicide prevention and resource organization, and he participated in the "Out of the Darkness Overnight Walks" organized by the American Foundation for Suicide Prevention.

That was helpful for Gary. So was reaching out for support from other fathers who had suffered the same loss. His wife seemed to gain more from her contact with other moms, but he understood that this was just a typical example of how guys don't easily forge the emotional bonds that women seem to do so naturally.

> **Insight for Loved Ones: After someone you love takes his own life, it's hard to know how to answer the question, "How many kids do you have?" or "How many siblings do you have?" If you include the one you've lost, you feel the need to explain, which is painful. If you don't include them, you feel like you're betraying them. Either way, it hurts.**

Gary just keeps finding his own way to go on, even as grief rises up when he receives graduation notices or wedding invitations from his son's peers. He still can't look at the photos of the last few years of Sam's life, but he can allow himself to revisit the fond memories of playing golf together or coaching his son's youth basketball team. He has come to appreciate any sign of healing. As he explains, "These days I can say that at least I feel normal more often than I used to."

### Biblical Insight:

Our lives are precious to God, and He confirms this truth in Psalm 116 and 34.

### Scripture:

**Psalm 34:18 NIV**

*Precious in the sight of the Lord is the death of his faithful servants.*

## Hammering on Us from all Angles

Sometimes it seems like life is just waiting to hit us from every angle. Let's take a look at the example of Ross to see how that can work.

After meeting me at a men's retreat, Ross invited me for coffee at an upscale hotel. As he began to talk, it was clear that things were not going very well for Ross at all. He was just barely holding on to his upper-level position at a major firm in the financial sector. "On top of that," he said, "my wife is threatening to leave me."

"Man, that's got to be hard," I told Ross. "I'll try to help you in any way I can."

For starters, I encouraged him to talk more about what happened so that he could process his feelings over his wife kicking him out of the house. As it turned out, there was a lot going on there. Ross had watched his dad tumble from being a bigshot to living a destitute life in a trailer, and now he had to acknowledge a fear that this one career setback would send him hurtling in his own out-of-control downward spiral. He did end up losing his job, but he was able to get up on his feet and fight for a two-year severance package, which gave him the cushion he needed to launch his own company.

Another part of Ross's story was that he had a drinking problem. I asked a friend of mine, a highly successful businessman who was twenty-plus years sober from drugs and alcohol, to lay out a plan to help Ross get sober. On the marriage front, this friend also talked directly with Ross's wife to acknowledge the craziness Ross had caused, but also to ask her to hang in there for just a little while longer. He suggested that Ross move out to take the stress away from his wife and to help Ross and his wife find a path to weather their storm and rebuild their union.

Ross was doing what he could by himself to control the damage from his drinking problem, but he wasn't making the healthy choice to commit to a recovery program to get sober and stay sober. Although alcoholism is not an addiction I have dealt with personally, I've had enough experience in 12-Step recovery programs to recognize that the process of choosing recovery can take time, with many stops and starts, before it takes hold. I told Ross that I was not giving up on him. Over time, I gained enough of his trust that he confided something else about his childhood: he had been sexually abused as a boy.

This news put a very different spin on what Ross was going through. I knew there was a pretty good chance that his drinking problem was a symptom of unresolved trauma from his sexual abuse, and that double-shot of loss just added fuel to the fire. To really get the help he needed, he would not only need to get sober but eventually face the trauma of being abused. He hasn't gotten there yet, but I'm hopeful that his healing will continue to unfold over time. I'm always hopeful that any man dealing with trauma and loss will find his way to a healthier, more satisfying life.

**Scripture:**

**1 Peter 5:8-11 MSG**

*Keep a cool head. Stay alert. The Devil is poised to pounce, and would like nothing better than to catch you napping. Keep your guard up. You're not the only ones plunged into these hard times. It's the same with Christians all over the world. So keep a firm grip on the faith. The suffering won't last forever. It won't be long before this generous God who has great plans for us in Christ—eternal and glorious plans they are!—will have you put together and on your feet for good. He gets the last word; yes, He does.*

## Biblical Insight:

## A biblical example of loss and abandonment

There are many examples of people going through loss, rejection, and abandonment in the Bible, but one of the most prevalent examples is Job. The loss he experienced is unbearable and unimaginable.

## Story:

## Job 1:1-20 MSG

*Job was a man who lived in Uz. He was honest inside and out, a man of his word, who was totally devoted to God and hated evil with a passion. He had seven sons and three daughters. He was also very wealthy—seven thousand head of sheep, three thousand camels, five hundred teams of oxen, five hundred donkeys, and a huge staff of servants—the most influential man in all the East!*

*His sons used to take turns hosting parties in their homes, always inviting their three sisters to join them in their merrymaking. When the parties were over, Job would get up early in the morning and sacrifice a burnt offering for each of his children, thinking, "Maybe one of them sinned by defying God inwardly." Job made a habit of this sacrificial atonement, just in case they'd sinned.*

*One day when the angels came to report to God, Satan, who was the Designated Accuser, came along with them. God singled out Satan and said, "What have you been up to?"*

*Satan answered God, "Going here and there, checking things out on earth."*

*God said to Satan, "Have you noticed my friend Job? There's no one quite like him—honest and true to his word, totally devoted to God and hating evil."*

*Satan retorted, "So do you think Job does all that out of the sheer goodness of his heart? Why, no one ever had it so good! You pamper him like a pet, make sure nothing bad ever happens to him or his family or his possessions, bless everything he does—he can't lose!*

*"But what do you think would happen if you reached down and took away everything that is his? He'd curse you right to your face, that's what."*

*God replied, "We'll see. Go ahead—do what you want with all that is his. Just don't hurt him." Then Satan left the presence of God.*

*Sometime later, while Job's children were having one of their parties at the home of the oldest son, a messenger came to Job and said, "The oxen were plowing and the donkeys grazing in the field next to us when Sabeans attacked. They stole the animals and killed the field hands. I'm the only one to get out alive and tell you what happened."*

*While he was still talking, another messenger arrived and said, "Bolts of lightning struck the sheep and the shepherds and fried them—burned them to a crisp. I'm the only one to get out alive and tell you what happened."*

*While he was still talking, another messenger arrived and said, "Chaldeans coming from three directions raided the camels and massacred the camel drivers. I'm the only one to get out alive and tell you what happened."*

*While he was still talking, another messenger arrived and said, "Your children were having a party at the home of the oldest brother when a tornado swept in off the desert and struck the house. It collapsed on the young people and they died. I'm the only one to get out alive and tell you what happened."*

*Job got to his feet, ripped his robe, shaved his head...*

As we have been seeing throughout this chapter, the process of addressing your trauma and loss may follow many twists and turns. You identify something that isn't working in your life, and you make a commitment to do what it takes to get better by dealing with that trauma. Then, at some point you discover that, surprise, there's another trauma or loss crying out for your attention.

And you just keep following the trail. Because that trail will lead to a happier and more satisfying life.

**Prayer:**

Father,

Help me to be of sound mind. Give me the grace to stay alert. The devil would like nothing more than to catch me off guard.

I'm not the only one plunged into these hard times. It's the same with Christians all over the world, so give me the grace to be strong in faith. This suffering won't last forever. It won't be long before You place me back on my feet for good. You get the last word concerning my life! In Jesus' name,

Amen.

# 7

## MEN EXPERIENCE MEDICAL TRAUMA

*Forty percent of all males will be diagnosed with cancer sometime intheir lifetimes.*

- The American Cancer Society

Men don't like to go to the doctor. That's another one of those generalizations you hear all the time about guys. We don't like to get check-ups, and we don'tseek medical help when some kind of symptom is telling us thatsomething could be/might be/ probably is wrong. We suck it up. We wait and wait until the problem is so big that we don't have any choice but to deal with it. Then, when we find ourselves face to face with some medical provider, and he or she starts asking us a bunch of questions, we shade the truth or minimize reality.

Do you think there's any truth to this kind of generalization? Has it ever been true for you?

When it comes to keeping close tabs on my physical health, I confess to being one of those guys for much of my life. I didn't really change my ways until I found myself knee deep in something that strikes millions of men at one time or another. It's what I call medical trauma.

It was the spring of 2017, the year I would turn fifty, and I had a sense that something was wrong. I didn't tell anyone why, of course, but I made an appointment to see a doctor for a physical. Sitting in the waiting room that day, I was thinking that I probably had not had a thorough physical since I was nineteen or twenty years old and still playing basketball, unless you count those quickie exams they give you when you change health care plans.

In the examination room, the doctor, a former hockey player, asked me one of those basic questions: "Have you had any bleeding in your stools recently?"

"Well, uh, sometimes," I admitted.

"Matt, you're almost fifty. It's a good time for you to get a colonoscopy," he said.

The dreaded procedure was scheduled for three months later, and during those ninety days I was naturally hoping that the blood would just go away on its own so I could cancel the test. I mean, who wants a doctor sticking something up your butt, right? Unfortunately, the blood was still showing up. Now I was starting to get just a little bit nervous.

Of course, any concern over a possible health crisis was no excuse to slow down at work. At that time, I was steering Helping Men Heal, an organization that I had launched. We had a major roundtable coming up, and that consumed most of my time and energy. I tried to forget about that little medical test on the horizon.

Test day arrived on the day the roundtable was to begin. So, immediately after being introduced as the CEO of the organization hosting this major event, I hurried off stage and reported for my colonoscopy. The next day I was dealing with a challenging issue that had popped up in the middle of the roundtable when I got a series of phone messages from a number I didn't recognize. Naturally, I ignored it. I went home that night, figuring that I would check to see if the results from the medical test had come in, only to find my wife already in our downstairs office. She was crying.

"It's cancer," she said.

That was Friday evening, so I would not have the chance to talk to the doctor until Monday. That meant that I had the entire weekend to think about this bad news. My wife, who is highly supportive of me, happens to be highly analytical and quick to plunge into research. In this situation, the information that she uncovered about colorectal cancer wasn't good: the overall survival rate for rectal cancer is about sixty-five percent. Even for Stage II and Stage III cancer, there was about a thirty percent chance of not surviving five years.

"Aw, those are just statistics," I responded, pretending not to be scared. "That's not me."

Statistics also tell us that close to half of all men will face some form of cancer in their lifetime. More than seven million men will specifically be diagnosed with colorectal cancer. I was about to take a seat on a roller-coaster ride that a huge number of guys like me wind up riding. All this came as a big surprise to me, since I didn't know that this trauma bus, the medical trauma bus, even existed.

As a sexual abuse survivor, with anal penetration part of my abuse, I was scared of the testing around rectal/colorectal cancer and concerned that it would start a series of intrusive testing in that area for the rest of my life. "This sucks," I said to myself.

It also sucked that I had planned a big turning-fifty birthday party for October 13, with a couple hundred friends coming in from near and far. I had to cancel that big bash. I was going to go through a bunch more tests, and who knew where that was going to lead? Probably the hardest thing to process was what one doctor told me right at the beginning. He said that this was a slow growing cancer, and that most likely the cancer had been growing inside of me for around seven years. Something about that felt very upsetting.

**Scripture:**

**Jeremiah 33:6 NIV**

*Nevertheless, I will bring health and healing to it; I will heal my people and will let them enjoy abundant peace and security.*

## The Cancer Roller-Coaster

While they went about giving me the CT scan and the MRI and every other test with some set of letters attached to it, it was unclear for a while whether I had Stage II or Stage III cancer. Either way, I had to strap myself into my seat and start riding through the treatments:

Two months of radiation, delivered five days a week until two days before Christmas.

Six months of chemotherapy. I had a port inserted in my chest so that every two minutes, more chemo could be pumped into me. This went on all night, and I could hear it all the time. I couldn't even take a shower. I grew to hate the sound of the pump putting a little bit of chemo into my system every two minutes, as it just reminded me that I was sick.

Major surgery to remove the tumor. The surgeon was nice enough to inform me that the type of surgery he was doing on me would register a 9.5 out of 10 on the Richter scale of surgeries. Well, I always did like to do things in a big way.

Feeding tubes down my nose. They sent me home four days after surgery because, after your stomach shuts down from surgery, it's supposed to wake up in three or four days. Initially we thought it did, but we soon discovered that mine didn't wake up for two weeks. For several days, I couldn't eat anything but ice. Enter the feeding tubes.

According to my surgeon, this only happens to five percent of those that have this surgery, where your stomach doesn't wake up for several days; well, I ended up as a five percenter.

Pills, pumps and shots administered right in my penis, and anything else we could come up with to try to combat the erectile dysfunction that I suddenly and pretty unexpectedly found myself in. My surgeon mentioned that there was a twenty-five percent chance that this could happen, as they had to cut through some nerves in the process of removing the cancer. I liked my chances but wound up on the bad side of those stats too.

Before getting cancer, I always thought Viagra commercials were a big joke. Even while I was undergoing radiation treatment, I assumed things would just naturally carry on the way they always had. Ha, the joke was on me. I learned that erectile dysfunction (ED) is *real*. The first couple of weeks, with all those catheters, I didn't really notice it. Then I took that test where the higher the number you score, the more functionality you have in that vital part of your anatomy. I scored all zeroes. The doctors told me, "Your functionality could come back, but then again it might never come back." Not the diagnosis that any male wants to hear.

I had to swing into action quickly and aggressively on that front. I also had to wear diapers at least half the time up until recently, because your body has to re-learn what's natural and what holds it in.

What I probably struggled with the most, as many do, was having an ileostomy bag for what ended up being nearly eight months. They shut down my plumbing to let the effects of the surgery on that area of my life heal. So that means pooping out of a bag that's attached to the side of my stomach. It affected everything. I found myself dumping that bag several times a day in every type of bathroom toilet you could imagine. That was weird and a bit gross sometimes, as many businesses take very poor care of their public bathrooms. But the hard part was continuing to work and work with the bag too. As CEO and primary key, big-client salesperson for our company, I was frequently out traveling to meet with people. I was always paranoid that they'd hear the bag fill up, because the bag had its own version of farting that could be embarrassing, not to mention that it had a different kind of smell to it.

Everything that I was trying to work around constantly reminded me that I was sick. I was also disturbed by another piece of news handed to me in my post-surgical haze. My tumor was bigger than what they had expected, and all that radiation and chemo I had been receiving had absolutely no impact on it. Zero. Nada. That meant that I would be having…

Four more months of chemo. Only this time they had to up the amount of chemo pumping into me. After this second round of chemo and a six-week break, they took out the bag and performed another round of surgery. At least this one didn't make it up to 9.5 on the Richter scale. When you're dealing with medical trauma, though, sometimes the biggest shock waves don't come from what they do to you; they come from the news they tell you.

Two weeks before the surgical procedure to remove the bag, a routine test to monitor whether the cancer might be coming back revealed something under my ribs. Had the cancer spread? The doctor shared the results with several colleagues but didn't have a definitive answer for my wife to our most important questions: did my cancer come back, did it spread, was it a new form of cancer, was it nothing? It was a time of uncertainty, and waiting to hear the answers created trauma for both of us. Even when we were in pre-op, as I was sitting there on the table waiting for the surgery to take out the bag, I still didn't know whether or not I had more cancer. Finally, just a half-hour before surgery, I got the verdict: no cancer. Hearing that, combined with getting rid of the poop bag, was a *huge* double-shot of relief for both of us.

But I still couldn't get off the cancer roller-coaster. When I had been on it almost a year, it was time for another colonoscopy. This time, the stuff they gave me to drink to prepare for the test apparently didn't clean me out well enough. That was news to me because when you're basically pooping water, you'd think you're good to go. Anyway, they did a repeat colonoscopy two days later and the doctor, who admitted later that he usually doesn't do such a thing, stuck a scope up my small intestine to take a peek and see if anything was there. He saw something that made him order a biopsy, and a week later I saw the familiar phone number on my cell phone. Uh-oh. When the doctor calls as soon as the test results come back, you know it's bad.

"It's a carcinoid," he said. He explained that the carcinoid, which is a tumor, was in my small intestine. We discussed a few different options on how to address it, but in the end, it meant that it was time to schedule another surgery. Surprisingly, miraculously, the pre-surgery tests they kept taking led to a discovery that no one saw coming: the new cancer, which he described as sort of like an egg with no chicken yet, was gone. The surgery was off. Whew!

**Scripture:**

**Psalm 119:81-83, 88 TLB**

*I faint for your salvation; but I expect your help, for you have promised it. My eyes are straining to see your promises come true. When will you comfort me with your help? I am shriveled like a wineskin in the smoke, exhausted with waiting. But still I cling to your laws and obey them... In your kindness, spare my life; then I can continue to obey you.*

> **Insight for Loved Ones:** *The* roller-coaster of his medical trauma impacts his entire family. As a loved one, *fi*nd the emotional support, counseling, support groups, etc., that will help you deal with your own pain.

I went from knowing nothing about cancer to, along with my very research-oriented wife, learning a lot about this disease in its many forms that impacts both us as patients and our families and loved ones. The people I'm most amazed by, though, are all the doctors, nurses and specialists, the janitorial crews and others at the hospitals where I had my surgeries, at radiation oncology where I got my radiation treatments, with my oncologist, my surgeon, the lab techs testing my blood before my chemo treatments. Such amazing people. Their work is a calling for them and you can tell. They didn't treat me like a stat, they treated me like a family member that they were going to do whatever they could to help get better.

It wasn't what I and many of us fear: white coats dispelling jargon and coldly probing patients. In fact, my cancer surgeon, who has guided me through a majority of the big and scariest things, is someone I have been able to connect with personally. He's in a band that plays gigs in Portland from time to time. With my radio DJ background and my experience managing some bands back in the day, I get the "doing gigs" thing. My wife and I are going to watch him and his band play soon. Cancer is scary—I was going to say "but"—a*nd* there are great people who have dedicated their lives to do all they can to help you beat it.

**Scripture:**

**Romans 12:9, 10 MSG**

*Love from the center of who you are; don't fake it. Run for dear life from evil; hold on for dear life to good. Be good friends who love deeply...*

## The Insane Stress of Living with Cancer

When that surgery was called off, it felt like I had come to a place on the roller-coaster where you just slow down and chill before the next big plunge. Will this ride with cancer take me down on a wild and crazy dive again any time soon? No way to know. As anyone who has lived with cancer will tell you, you just learn to live with the uncertainty. And the upheaval. And the insane stress. That's what getting hit with a medical trauma does to you.

In my situation, my head was spinning with a sense that everything that shouldn't happen statistically was happening to me. That's because only five percent of those who undergo a surgery like mine find that their stomach does not wake up after a few days, and less than half of men who go through these kinds of cancer treatments wind up with erectile dysfunction.

It's one thing to wake up to the reality that you've got cancer, but when you just say "Oh, that sucks," you're not really thinking about the ED, the bag you wear, the sound of the chemo pumping into you and everything else that comes with the full package of medical trauma.

You also don't think about the trickle-down effect that seeps into other parts of your life. For me, I had to deal with the added stress of witnessing the company I had launched struggling to stay afloat. Right in the midst of some cancer treatment, I would get calls about how we were going to make payroll.

**Understanding Trauma Reminder: When you're *fi*ghting a medical trauma, the stress goes way beyond the physical challenges.**

My stress was showing up in lots of other ways. I went through a period where I tried to escape from the anxiety and fear by eating everything in sight, which led to a rapid thirty-pound weight gain. I also tried to bury myself in work, so I wouldn't have to sit around thinking about what was going to happen next on the medical front. By that time, I knew that these little side effects of my medical trauma were addictive practices and I had to take the time to deal with them. I'll talk about that more later, when I guide you along my own healing journey and the potential for healing for any male who has survived trauma or loss.

Medical trauma, whether it strikes us when we are young, middle- aged or older, impacts us on many layers and levels. With my cancer, I had to deal with my own emotions, which I did mostly by making daily videos in which I told my story in gritty detail and no-holds-barred language. At the same time, I faced the challenge of trying to manage the emotions of everybody else in my life.

My parents wanted to be involved in what was going on, and although they meant well, some of the words they spoke to me didn't exactly calm my nerves. I had to search for ways to allow them to participate in my support network while not being destructive to me. My wife and my two sons were also struggling. They loved me and were deeply concerned about my well-being, so it was difficult for them to see me hurting. I knew that they also must be concerned about the impact of my cancer on our economic state and all the other ways in which our whole family life was being turned upside-down. My adult daughter, who typically would call me every few weeks or so, was suddenly calling every day. My family suffered what I believe was/is vicarious trauma, witnessing me go through cancer diagnosis and treatment. I wasn't the only one on this roller-coaster.

When you're a guy dealing with medical trauma, it's easy to slip into a male way of approaching these challenges. That means shutting down your own needs and focusing on how you can help those you love deal with seeing you so vulnerable, which often leads to pretending you're not really vulnerable anyway. Living with medical trauma has been teaching me that I have to find ways to take care of myself first.

For me, it also helped to discover that so many men deal with cancer. It was another important reminder that I was not alone. It also reminded me that in my mission to help men deal with trauma, I had something else that I could talk about from first-hand experience. Hey, you've got to look at the positive side!

What else do I have to offer about how to hold your ground while riding this roller-coaster of medical trauma? Well, the first message I can give you is to take care of your body and get regular check- ups. And yeah, that means getting colonoscopies when doctors tell you it's time to do so. Let go of your avoidance strategy because you don't want someone touching your butt. I mean, you're going to be asleep while they do what they have to do anyway. Too many men wind up dealing with years of suffering, or even die prematurely, just because they were afraid of taking a medical test. Don't be one of them!

Medical trauma can strike at any time in our lives. It can arrive as one of the many types of cancer or in other forms. Men have heart attacks and strokes and get hit with diagnoses of all kinds of major illnesses, diseases or medical conditions that could potentially shake up their lives from top to bottom. It's just part of being alive.

**Biblical Insight:**

**A biblical example of a man tormented**

Job, one of the richest men in the world at that time, lost not only his children and all his possessions, but also his health.

**Job 2: 1-10 MSG**

*One day when the angels came to report to God, Satan also showed up. God singled out Satan, saying, "And what have you been up to?" Satan answered God, "Oh, going here and there, checking things out." Then God said to Satan, "Have you noticed my friend Job? There's no one quite like him, is there—honest and true to his word, totally devoted to God and hating evil? He still has a firm grip on his integrity! You tried to trick me into destroying him, but it didn't work."*

*Satan answered, "A human would do anything to save his life. But what do you think would happen if you reached down and took away his health? He'd curse you to your face, that's what."*

*God said, "All right. Go ahead—you can do what you like with him. But mind you, don't kill him."*

*Satan left God and struck Job with terrible sores. Job was ulcers and scabs from head to foot. They itched and oozed so badly that he took a piece of broken pottery to scrape himself, then went and sat on a trash heap, among the ashes.*

*His wife said, "Still holding on to your precious integrity, are you? Curse God and be done with it!"*

*He told her, "You're talking like an empty-headed fool. We take the good days from God—why not also the bad days?"*

*Not once through all this did Job sin. He said nothing against God.*

> **Understanding Trauma Reminder: When you're dealing with a medical trauma, you've got to take care of yourself emotionally, not just physically.**

If a medical event comes charging through your door, without knocking, I would recommend that you recognize that this isn't only a physical health issue and that the impact of your medical condition, whether actualized or something you suspect could be coming, can definitely cause trauma. Taking care of yourself in the middle of that trauma doesn't just mean listening to your doctors and doing everything on your end to help the healing process. That's definitely important. But it's just as important to deal with the emotional impact of medical trauma.

Find someone to talk to about what you're going through. Keep a journal, write a blog, make a video, do a podcast—find some way to process your fear, anxiety, or whatever else you find yourself in the middle of. Practice letting go of what you can't control and focus on what you can do to help yourself. If you have religious or spiritual beliefs, call upon them to help keep you anchored. Get into a support group; I did. I discovered that groups met regularly for cancer patients and family members of cancer patients. Reach out to others who have faced whatever particular kind of medical trauma has struck you. They're often very willing to share stories from down in the trenches. Oh, and take the time to read the second section of this book that we're about to begin.

**Biblical Insight:**

**Paul's perspective on suffering**

According to Paul, we do not suffer in vain. When we show the light of Jesus in spite of what's going on in our lives, God is able to give us the best possible outcome.

**Scripture:**

**2 Corinthians 4:7-18 MSG**

*If you only look at us, you might well miss the brightness. We carry this precious Message around in the unadorned clay pots of our ordinary lives. That's to prevent anyone from confusing God's incomparable power with us. As it is, there's not much chance of that. You know for yourselves that we're not much to look at.*

*We've been surrounded and battered by troubles, but we're not demoralized; we're not sure what to do, but we know that God knows what to do; we've been spiritually terrorized, but God hasn't left our side; we've been thrown down, but we haven't broken. What they did to Jesus, they do to us—trial and torture, mockery and murder; what Jesus did among them, he does in us—he lives! Our lives are at constant risk for Jesus' sake, which makes Jesus' life all the more evident in us. While we're going through the worst, you're getting in on the best!*

*We're not keeping this quiet, not on your life. Just like the psalmist who wrote, "I believed it, so I said it," we say what we believe. And what we believe is that the One who raised up the Master Jesus will just as certainly raise us up with you, alive. Every detail works to your advantage and to God's glory: more and more grace, more and more people, more and more praise!*

*So we're not giving up. How could we! Even though on the outside it often looks like things are falling apart on us, on the inside, where God is making new life, not a day goes by without his unfolding grace. These hard times are small potatoes compared to the coming good times, the lavish celebration prepared for us. There's far more here than meets the eye. The things we see now are here today, gone tomorrow. But the things we can't see now will last forever.*

## Turning onto the Healing Road

Okay, we've been spending a lot of time looking at the many kinds of traumas that men experience. To help you better understand what trauma is and what it does, I've provided many close-up shots of what it's like to suffer sexual trauma, physical trauma, verbal and emotional trauma, the suffering that comes from loss, rejection and abandonment, and now the common experience of medical trauma. I'm not going to pretend that this is a complete, all-bases-covered trauma list. There are many, many other trauma buses that could smack into you and knock you down, delivering their own kind of pain and suffering.

But, as I follow my mission of helping men heal from trauma, it's time to move on from talking about what trauma is and zero in on what you can do about it.

It's hard for anyone to take on any dose of trauma. It's especially hard for us men to wrap our heads and our arms around this whole business of actually *healing* from trauma. This is foreign or unfamiliar terrain for many of us, and it can be intimidating because it brings us smack up against many of those generalized beliefs about being a man we've been talking about.

My goal is to help you break down those walls of intimidation. I'm going to take the same kinds of close-up shots about my own experiences, and the wide world of other men seeking to heal from trauma, to open up the lens of awareness and understanding on what the road toward healing is all about.

Come along with me down that road now. See for yourself what it means to start breaking free from the shackles of trauma and to truly become unbound. I've got the GPS aligned with the route. Here we go.

**<u>Prayer:</u>**

Father,

As I live my life, I carry Your message inside me. I have been surrounded and battered by troubles, but I am not demoralized. When I am not sure what to do, You know what to do. You never left my side. When I was thrown down, You did not allow me to be broken. My life is at constant risk for Jesus' sake, which makes Jesus' life all the more evident in me. The Holy Spirit Who raised Jesus from the dead is raising me up from this death pit. Every detail works to my advantage and to God's glory! My testimony will reach more and more people and give You more and more praise.

So I refuse to give up! Even though on the outside it looks like things are falling apart for me, You are building new life. Not a day goes by that You don't shower me with Your grace. There's far more going on than meets the eye. The things I see now are here today and gone tomorrow. But the things I can't see now will last forever. In Jesus' name,

Amen.

# PART TWO
## MEN CAN HEAL FROM TRAUMA

# 8

## THE DOOR TO HEALING OPENS

### WITH AWARENESS, ACCEPTANCE AND ACTION

*"Although you are not responsible for all the things that you may have encountered to this point, you ARE responsible for what you DO about the hurt you feel."*

- Michael S. Figgers, *Healing the Hearts of Broken Men*

The first secret I can share with you about the road to recovery and healing from trauma is that it's not something marked with one big, bold-letter sign that says "Trauma Recovery," like a directional sign on an interstate or in an airport terminal. Even if such a sign existed, most guys would be too intimidated to follow it anyway. We'd just go some other way. Or we wouldn't be ready to identify the problem we're dealing with as "Trauma" in the first place.

So how does this process of seeking help and getting better actually work? Who or what is going to help show you the way? After spending the past twenty-eight years on my own road to healing and wholeness from all those traumas I told you about, I've come up with one description of what will open the door, pointing you where you need to be to launch your own healing path and start navigating your way toward a more peaceful, fulfilling and satisfying life. It's a simple three-step process:

1. Awareness 2. Acceptance 3. Action

**Awareness** just means that you're starting to recognize that something is not right in your life. It might be awareness of a particular form of trauma or loss that you picked up from something you came across in your day-to-day life. Something made the light switch on. Maybe the switch flicked on while you were reading the first half of this book, through the many traumas that we have been shining the spotlight on. But you don't have to be aware of a specific trauma to start getting help. You may find yourself just becoming aware of one of the many symptoms of trauma: an addiction, anxiety, depression, nightmares, flashbacks, a relationship in turmoil, a career or financial loss or crisis, doing something that put you in prison, etc. One way or another, you just have that sense that "something's messed up in my life."

> **Insight for Loved Ones:** It's natural that you may have seen the hurt, trauma, pain or addiction that he couldn't, but restrain yourself from saying "I told you so" and try to tune in to his new discoveries as he makes them.

**Acceptance** is the step that comes after you have learned something about physical trauma, sexual trauma, emotional trauma or any other trauma or symptom of trauma that describes your experience. You take this step when you *accept* that this trauma or symptom is real for you. You're going further than just saying, "Something's messed up in my life" by adding the phrase "and I have at least some idea about what it may be." You know you have a problem and it's not getting better. Slowly, you're beginning to put a name to that problem and saying, "Yeah, that's me."

**Action** is the third step of the process, and it's a critical piece of the puzzle. It's nice to know about a trauma or a symptom and accept that it very well may be something that describes what is troubling you. But if you don't take action to get help, you won't see any positive change in your life. That problem won't be going away just because you've named it.

I want to make an important point about this action step. With our training as men, we often fall into a belief that once we have identified a problem, we're just going to *beat* that problem. That usually takes the form of pushing the problem to the side and pretending it doesn't exist. You know, that whole manning up thing. Or we figure we can beat a problem like having an addiction by just upping our performance level somewhere else in life, like making a bunch of money or achieving a certain status. But this attempt at beating the problem just makes the problem get bigger, because beating the problem is not the same as *solving* the problem. And solving the problem leads to health and healing. That's the kind of action we're talking about in this A-A-A process.

Once you have decided to take action and you complete that first step to address a trauma or symptom of trauma in your life, the possibilities of how to get better just open up. For men, taking that first step might be the hardest thing we ever do. But I'm here to remind you that it also leads to the greatest rewards. I'm also here to provide you with information, guidance and understanding, gained from first-hand experience, that can make this whole idea of getting help for trauma something you're ready to sign on to and even embrace.

Of course, you know me well enough by now to realize that I'm not going to do this in a textbook, academic way. Nope. I'm just going to take out my camera again and zoom right in on how I went through the Awareness-Acceptance-Action cycle.

**Biblical Insight:**

**Paul demands actions of humility and love**

Paul also took the approach of Awareness-Acceptance-Action Cycle. He opened the eyes of Christians, showing them their fate (awareness). He served others so as not to detract from the Message of Christ (acceptance). Then he set into action the power of the Gospel with love and humility (action).

**Scripture:**

**1 Corinthians 9:20-27 MSG**

*I didn't take on their way of life. I kept my bearings in Christ—but I entered their world and tried to experience things from their point of view. I've become just about every sort of servant there is in my attempts to lead those I meet into a God-saved life. I did all this because of the Message. I didn't just want to talk about it; I wanted to be in on it!*

*You've all been to the stadium and seen the athletes race. Everyone runs; one wins. Run to win. All good athletes train hard. They do it for a gold medal that tarnishes and fades. You're after one that's gold eternally.*

*I don't know about you, but I'm running hard for the finish line. I'm giving it everything I've got. No lazy living for me! I'm staying alert and in top condition. I'm not going to get caught napping, telling everyone else all about it and then missing out myself.*

**1 Corinthians 16:15-16 MSG**

*Keep your eyes open, hold tight to your convictions, give it all you've got, be resolute, and love without stopping.*

## A Real Romeo

When I was in my early twenties, I was living a life that would have made lots of guys my age jealous. I had a super-cool day job and a company I started on the side that was becoming successful, and I was making good money for a kid who had not yet earned a college degree. I was becoming well known to a wide and appreciative audience. And women? Oh yeah! Though now I find it to be more embarrassing than anything else, I was definitely a player and proud of it back in the day.

Let me back up. I had lost my basketball scholarship at a small college in Portland but was making ends meet by working as a DJ. I had started doing that back in high school and had built up a reputation because I was *good*. See, I wouldn't just play the music, I would perform to the music. I'd dress up like Prince or Hammer and dance on top of speakers. During those days of performers like Prince and MC Hammer, I mastered the "Build and Slam" technique where you start out slow, then build the tempo and just slam it down. I'm telling you, I could make a place filled with hundreds of people just start pulsating.

I had one problem, though. To be a great DJ, I needed more records than I could afford to buy. I figured out a way around that. After learning that radio stations were routinely given tons of records to play and weren't allowed to sell them, I volunteered to take some of those excess records off their hands. Z100 in Portland was my primary go-to record provider. While jockeying for free records, I would sit around and watch and listen to the DJs on the radio. "I can do that," I said to myself, and before long

I convinced the station manager to give me a shot as an on-air personality. That was my big break!

By then, I had established my own DJ Company, Romeo Productions. My DJ name was Romeo because that's what one of the girls I dated in college called me. Anyway, when I got on this Top 40 and rap station, they told me I needed a last name because I wasn't somebody like Prince or Madonna who could go by just one name. They asked me my favorite color, and when I told them it was blue, they made my last name Bleu, as in bleu cheese. Soon Romeo Bleu was tearing up the airwaves, and the exposure ramped up my DJ business, where I was making 200 bucks or more an hour doing school dances, corporate parties, weddings, and other events!

Like many young men getting a taste of success, I wanted more. I was going to open up nightclubs all over the country and then expand beyond U.S. borders. I'd buy myself a yacht and fill it up with shows and parties, with lots of women running around.

**Scripture:**

**Proverbs 16:9 NIV**

*In their hearts humans plan their course,*

*but the Lord establishes their steps.*

### Finding a Book by "Accident"

On the outside, my life looked like great. But on the inside, the picture was different. Very different. For one thing, I was working too many hours a week to count and was not taking care of myself. I didn't drink, but I was a total sugar junkie. For another thing, I had a two-year-old daughter with a woman I had not married and was no longer living with, and I didn't get to see my little girl nearly as much as I wanted. Then, in the midst of all that "fun" of sleeping around, as I mentioned earlier, I got a young woman pregnant. After that happened, in the summer of 1991, I was a wreck.

I was living alone, just coming back to my own little world after all those one-night stands. Looking back, I am able to recognize that this whole Romeo persona just wasn't me. It was just a way to try to cover my low self-esteem, a byproduct of sexual abuse.

What I did know at the time was that even though I was getting lots of sex, I couldn't keep my hands off of pornography. This was way before Internet porn. It all started by my looking at the underwear and bra ads in J.C. Penney and Sears catalogs as a teenager, and from there it just took off. Lots of my friends had all of the adult magazines. But no matter how much real sex and imaginary sex I was having, it wasn't enough. Not enough frequency, not enough variety—just not enough. I felt some kind of magnetic pull toward pornography that I just couldn't fight off.

The seeds of that first step of Awareness were being planted. Then, by "accident," I happened to find myself in a library one day looking at a book that just happened to have information about guys being addicted to pornography and what to do about it. Huh, that was an interesting book to stumble upon.

**Biblical Insight:**

God confirms His word again in in both Proverbs 16 and Proverbs 19.

**Scripture:**

**Proverbs 19:21 NIV**

*Many are the plans in a person's heart,*

*but it is the Lord's purpose that prevails.*

Now I was beginning to cross over from the Awareness step to the Acceptance step. I was not yet identifying the trauma that was causing my addiction to pornography, but that would come soon enough.

> **Healing Trauma Reminder: It doesn't matter how you first become aware of your trauma or some symptom of trauma, only that you pay attention to it.**

I wasn't yet ready to move on to the Action step on this addiction. But I did want to start cleaning up my life. That meant focusing my attention on trying to make a real relationship with the mother of my two-year-old daughter. In the fall of 1991, she and I started talking again. Within a few months we made the decision to get married.

## "You're Home"

We set the big date for the 4th of July. Before entering into a marriage agreement, I was aware enough to know that if I really wanted to make this thing work, I needed to take action on my awareness of my addiction to pornography. A resource book pointed me to 12-Step recovery meetings that could help with that, and I found one held at a church in southeast Portland.

I had circled the night of May 1st to attend my first meeting, but before that day arrived, I got a DJ gig the same night. Now

I wasn't going to go to that meeting, and maybe that first excuse would lead to a series of excuses that would keep me from ever getting help. But God intervened; he had other plans. My DJ assignment got cancelled, something that almost never happened. I figured, "What the heck, I'm not working, I might as well go to that meeting."

That night, I walked into my first 12-Step meeting. It was more than that; it was the first time I had ever taken any action step to get help for any problem like this in my life.

When I entered the church meeting room and the other guys there began sharing their stories about how they were addicted to pornography, I said, "Whoa! This is the same stuff that I have been doing and can't stop." I felt the truth of a common saying in 12- Step circles: "You're home."

**Healing Trauma Reminder: It can really help to find a place where it's safe to share your secrets, as well as a path that others have followed to get better.**

Everything that was being shared in that room just made sense. I also quickly understood that in 12-Step groups, men can talk about the kinds of things that men just don't talk about. It was safe, safe to share your secrets. In most environments, men are terrified to reveal their secrets because they assume that other men, and women too, just won't be able to deal with them. They will be judged, criticized or ostracized. I don't think women usually have the same level of fear. Being in a 12-Step group as a guy, however, you learn that the playing field gets levelled. Men can talk as openly as women do, and they won't be judged. That's a big eye- opening experience for men, considering that most of us don't even have close male friends and, with the guys we do talk to, the conversation is usually limited to sports, work, money or our home and gadgets.

## One Action Step Leads to Another

I felt so comfortable in that 12-Step group for addiction to pornography that I accepted an invitation by two guys there to check out a men-only therapy group to deal with this problem. This group was facilitated by a man-and-woman team. Again, I heard familiar stories of challenges and struggles. Again, I felt safe to reveal my secrets. And again, there was no judgment, only support. Total support.

It was just the kind of support I needed, so different from that emotionally abusive high school basketball coach who kept finding more things *wrong* with me and never validated anything I was doing right. It all added up to a great start! I reached out for help for a problem that I knew was messing up my life, and I was immediately guided into how to start making it better. Not only that, but I was surrounded by other men who understood what I was going through because they had been travelling down the same road. And when I didn't jump through all the hoops right away, they didn't threaten to kick me out of "the club."

I had found the place where I needed to be, a place where I could learn as much as I could about this one problem. A place where I could begin the long process of healing and recovery. A place where I would have a shot to turn my life around.

**Scripture:**

**1 Peter 3: 8-12 MSG**

*Be agreeable, be sympathetic, be loving, be compassionate, be humble. That goes for all of you, no exceptions. No retaliation. No sharp-tongued sarcasm. Instead, bless—that's your job, to bless. You'll be a blessing and also get a blessing.*

*Whoever wants to embrace life
and see the day fill up with good,
Here's what you do:
Say nothing evil or hurtful;
Snub evil and cultivate good;
run after peace for all you're worth.
God looks on all this with approval,
listening and responding well to what He's asked...*

> **Insight for Loved Ones:** If you feel frustrated by the amount of time he's spending away from you and your family while engaging in healing from trauma or recovery from an addiction, try to be patient; the time will likely rebalance after a while.

Notice that I did not arrive in this place because I had identified myself as a survivor of some kind of male trauma. What led me to the starting gate was one of many possible symptoms of trauma: an addiction to pornography. As I mentioned earlier, that's typically how it works for most men. The "click" that sets us on the path to healing is likely to be a crisis or an addiction, whether that is to alcohol or drugs or one of the process addictions like pornography or gambling or gaming. Some obsessive habit or activity is throwing our lives out of control. That may be all that we can see and identify as the problem, but it's enough to jump-start the healing process.

The click also can come when a man faces a crisis. There's something about our partners muttering the words, "I'm going to leave you if you don't deal with (fill in the blank)" that somehow has the force needed to nudge us toward our first action step to get help with a problem. A crisis also might take the form of getting fired, dropping out of school or having a business collapse. Or maybe it's the death of a loved one, especially our spouse or a child.

**Healing Trauma Reminder: Reaching out for help in the middle of a crisis can open a door to healing trauma that you suffered a long time before that crisis.**

For some men, getting thrown into prison is the crisis that wakes them up and starts the Awareness-Acceptance-Action cycle. With prisoners, though, the action steps are often delayed while they are still incarcerated. Prisoners may be offered counseling and addiction recovery services, but they often fear that if they reach out for that kind of help, they will be labelled as weak. Any prisoner who chooses to attend a support group for addiction to pornography is immediately ridiculed: "You want to get pornography out of your life? Man, why are you doing that? Oh, and if you're really going to get rid of your porn, can I have it?"

As I mentioned earlier, attitudes like that explain why it's usually more helpful to work with men transitioning to life outside of prison. The step of taking action is a difficult one for those still incarcerated. That doesn't mean it's impossible for men to begin healing work while incarcerated; many do. It's just more challenging. Facing possible ridicule is one reason, but probably more concerning is the idea of engaging in trauma healing work in a place where actual and vicarious trauma is happening all the time. Healing from trauma is big, and so is doing it in a way that isn't retraumatizing. Once out of prison, the time is often more fitting for them to look at why they did what they did to land in prison in the first place, and what may be triggering their behavior. When they are guided toward awareness and acceptance of something that has hurt them, they may begin the process of getting to the root of their trauma and pain. Then they'll be better able to heal from what hurt them, so they don't have to hurt others anymore.

Physical symptoms also can get men moving toward healing, especially when we seek medical treatment and the physician treating us is wise enough to recognize that there may be some emotional or psychological issue contributing to the problem. That was the case with a guy I assisted who was wrestling with Parkinson's disease. He was getting treatment for injuries suffered when he was attacked by three guys with a baseball bat. At one point, the doctor treating him advised him that if he wanted to enhance the outcome of a possible new surgery that could help to heal his physical injuries in the short term and reduce some of his Parkinson's symptoms in the long term, he should address the underlying emotional trauma from the attack that caused those injuries.

## Following the Call

Whatever it is that may be driving you toward seeking help, follow the call. Reach out for help or guidance for that one problem or challenge that you have identified. Take that bold first action step. Feel the support of other men (and women, too, if they are part of the picture) who have suffered and survived the same kind of problem you're facing, or who have the professional expertise to guide you toward healing.

Reaching out for help is scary, but it helps when you know you're not alone. Like fellow soldiers in a squad or platoon, or teammates on a sports team, other guys who are in the same battle as you will give you the strength and courage to do what you need to do. You just keep following the trail that you find yourself walking on.

That's how it worked for me. I was led to that first 12-Step meeting for addiction to pornography, and from there I was led to a therapeutic group for men seeking recovery. The trail didn't stop there. Not by a long shot. The pain I had been dragging around since forever was not going away. I was just becoming more aware of it.

> **Insight for Loved Ones:** If you read the Alcoholics Anonymous or AA Big Book and substitute the word alcohol for whatever addiction your loved one may be struggling with, you'll gain insight into his particular struggle and the solution.

At Christmas, the mother of my daughter gave me a book. By that time, I'd shared some of my history with her. She knew enough about my background to have an idea of what I was dealing with, or trying not to deal with. Still being prone to denying or minimizing the trauma that was very real in my life, I didn't read the book right away.

That book was *The Sexual Healing Journey: A Guide for Survivors of Sexual Abuse* by Wendy Maltz. I put it aside for a while until one night when I was DJ'ing at a wedding. I had always found weddings boring, and this one was in some VFW hall in the middle of nowhere. With time to kill, I sat in my van and took out that book. I started reading it, and I kept on reading it even after the wedding.

I discovered, in the midst of reading this book, that I was a sexual abuse survivor! I learned that I didn't do something wrong when I was growing up, I got abused. It wasn't my fault. It was something huge that happened to me that changed my life.

At that moment, I recognized that I really had suffered trauma. And the more I read, the better I understood the many invisible wounds that sexual trauma had imprinted in my life. Sexual trauma had messed up all my feelings about sex and my response to it. Sexual trauma left me carrying layers and layers of shame. Sexual trauma crippled my ability to trust anybody.

Wendy Maltz's words took me right into Awareness of what sexual trauma is all about and Acceptance of the reality that I was a sexual abuse survivor. And it guided me right into the final phase: Action.

Wendy Maltz wrote, "The only way out of the pain is straight ahead." Okay, I was fully on board. Now that I knew that I really was a sexual abuse survivor and that it had messed up my life, I just needed to find where to go to do something about that.

**Scripture:**

**Romans 5:3-5 TLB**

*...when we run into problems and trials, for we know that they are good for us—they help us learn to be patient. And patience develops strength of character in us and helps us trust God more each time we use it until finally our hope and faith are strong and steady. Then, when that happens, we are able to hold our heads high no matter what happens and know that all is well, for we know how dearly God loves us, and we feel this warm love everywhere within us because God has given us the Holy Spirit to fill our hearts with His love.*

**Prayer:**

Father,

The only way out of pain is straight ahead through Your grace and Your word. I know that because I'm Yours, good is waiting for me.

Patience develops my strength of character and helps me to trust You more each time I use it. I will be able to hold my head up high no matter what happens. All is well with me because I know how dearly You love me. You have given me the Holy Spirit to fill my heart with Your love. Thank You, Father. In Jesus' name, Amen.

## 9

## BREAKING FREE FROM THE SHACKLES BY "GOING THERE"

*"Everyone needs someone to talk to. Someone who can be fully trusted, and, in the case of trauma victims, someone who can help them through the tough times."*

- Randy Boyd, *Healing the Man Within*

It's hard for most men to decide to engage a support group, counseling or psychotherapy. First, we resist the idea that we really need that kind of help. As men, we're supposed to be strong. We should be able to solve all our own problems, to figure things out for ourselves. Counseling may be okay for women, but it's just not manly, you know.

**Scripture:**

**Proverbs 13:10 TLB**

*Pride leads to arguments; be humble, take advice, and become wise.*

Second, we're a little intimidated about what will happen *if* we ever do decide to get professional help. We're going to have to talk about ourselves and our . . . *feelings?* Whoa, that's foreign territory for most men right there. If we say yes to counseling, we'll have to "go there," which most men imagine as a dark road of revealing secrets and sharing emotions that we don't even know we have.

Then we're supposed to somehow make sense of all those feelings, pull all the pieces of our lives apart, and put them all back together again in some perfect new picture frame. We're expected to totally change who we are and how we live, right? Crazy!

I admit I had some of those thoughts when I learned that I was a survivor of sexual trauma and began to understand that being abused had led to so much destructive behavior in my life. I knew that I had to take the leap from going to group meetings to a one-on-one, full-spotlight-on-me battle plan. But it was still scary. Especially the part about dealing with feelings when I didn't even know what feelings were.

## Telling the "Hole" Story

Sharing some of my secrets in those 12-Step meetings made the ride to the next step on my healing trail a little easier. Some people say that if you're going to get help to deal with trauma and its effects, you've got to learn to tell the "whole story," the complete story, not just the parts that you think will be acceptable while hiding those you want to keep secret. But I was already learning that it's not just about telling the *whole* story, it's also about telling the *hole* story.

You may be thinking, "Wait, what? The *hole* story? What the heck are you talking about there, Matt?" Telling the "hole story" means not just reciting facts and recapping all the bad stuff that happened to you, like ESPN's *SportsCenter* showing all the key highlights of a big football game. It's about getting to the parts about the vulnerability and the pain. You know, the stuff that really hurts and why it hurts. The "hole story" is all about the trauma that left a crater-sized hole in your life.

Once you get that out in the open, you can make more sense of it. You can see why things have been the way they've been, and, with professional help and guidance, you can begin to see how they can be different. Instead of feeling like your life is totally out of control, you uncover the possibility of actually taking charge of your life. I got my feet wet in that process in 12-Step meetings, so I thought maybe/possibly/hypothetically I could do it more with a counselor.

## A Recovery Church

Other factors also helped give me the confidence to reach out for this kind of help. East Hill Church, where I'd visited six months earlier through an invitation from my former neighbors and my mom, was becoming a much bigger part of my life. I went to a full Sunday service and then another, and by the time they got to the part about inviting anyone who was ready to accept Jesus as their savior to stand up, I bolted out of my seat.

After being just an Easter and Christmas type of church-goer before, God had fully entered my life. From that point on through today, my faith has remained a constant positive force in my life. I recognize that religion may not play a central role in everybody's pursuit of a healthier and more satisfying life, but I just want to be open and honest about how it has worked that way for me.

I found the East Hill Church congregation of about 8,000 people a really supportive community, and Ted Roberts, the pastor, became a role model for me. Ted took a sincere interest in my life and kept reassuring me that I mattered, that I had value, that God cared about me. You can bet those were comforting messages for somebody who was still hearing echoes of his abuser telling him, "You're nothing, a waste, a zero!"

East Hill happened to be a recovery church. They offered many opportunities to pursue healing from all kinds of traumas and problems, and I jumped right into many of them, including a group for adult children of dysfunctional families. I figured that my family qualified there, with a home environment where my mom and my dad did not protect me from my abusers. Nor did they take the time and steps to nurture me after they learned at least part of the truth of what had been happening to me.

So, I had some experience in telling the *whole* story and the *hole* story. I had the support of a loving God and a caring community. I had the awareness and acceptance of being a survivor of sexual trauma. And then I had one little extra push: my marriage to my daughter's mom fell apart.

In our own ways, she and I had at least tried to make it work. But today, long after all the finger-pointing and the pain, and after a whole lot of healing work, I would say that we just weren't capable of building and maintaining a healthy marriage together. And I knew that I needed counseling to figure out my own problems.

**Scripture:**

**Proverbs 15:22 ESV**

***Without counsel plans fail, but with advisors they succeed.***

## How Does Counseling Work?

I needed to talk about and better understand what happened to me when I was sexually abused and how it kept affecting me. But I still had this fear that when I actually explained what happened, no one would believe me. Or they would invalidate my experience. Or they would think I was weak. There was no way that fear was going to stop me from doing what I knew I needed to do, however.

My first step was to answer the question, "How do you find a counselor?" Today, anyone looking for professional help to deal with trauma or loss can simply go online and sort through a comprehensive list of licensed counselors, psychotherapists, psychiatrists, social workers and other healthcare professionals, or they can seek referrals from their doctor, their pastor or others they know and trust. But in those pre-Internet days, I couldn't google my way to the information I needed. I just picked up my phone book and looked up "Sexual Abuse Counselors." My search landed on one name.

The counselor's office was located in Lake Oswego, a wealthy suburb of Portland where you would seldom find people of color. That didn't deter me either. I made the phone call, set up an appointment and got there on time. That showed how important this really was to me, because I was always a little late to pretty much anything and everything in my life. My mom would often say that I was born two weeks late and never caught up.

"So why are you here, Matt?" the male counselor asked after I sat down.

"Well, like I said on the phone, I read this book that made me realize I was sexually abused and . . . well . . . I guess I need help for that," I explained. "But I don't know the first thing about how this counseling thing works."

"I understand," he said. "Let me see how I can best explain it. Each of us has a closet in our lives. Inside that closet is all our unresolved pain: hurts and traumas of all kinds, losses, failures, labels, lies, disappointments. Most of us have some scary and smelly skeletons in that closet."

I nodded my head.

"My job is to give you the encouragement and the tools to crack open the door to that dark, smelly, scary closet just a little bit," my counselor went on. "Together, we'll reach in and pull out just one of those scary things. We'll let some light come through it. We'll talk about what it is, and I'll help you work through the memories, the feelings, the beliefs and the impact it has had on your life. The goal is to reach a point where that thing is not so scary anymore.

"When we meet that goal, we'll push that scary thing off to the side. You'll get a well-deserved rest, take some deep breaths. Then we'll crack open the door to that closet again. Maybe then it will seem just a little less smelly, a little less scary. And we'll take the next thing out of that closet and follow the same process. We'll keep going this way until that dark, scary closet is pretty empty."

> **Healing Trauma Reminder: When you go to any counselor or therapist for the *first* time, write down how the process is going to work and remember: their job is to help you get better; your job is to do the hard work that is asked of you to get better.**

I was blown away by this whole description of counseling and how it could help me deal with the trauma from sexual abuse and start making my life better. It sounded like just what I needed, but it also sounded like it was going to take a lot of time. And cost me a whole lot of money, which I didn't have. I just assumed that counseling was something you went to once or twice and you'd get everything you needed.

I had no doubt that this counselor had the skill and experience to guide me where I needed to go. But I had to respectfully tell him that I just couldn't afford Lake Oswego rates and would need to find a helper who was a lot less expensive.

This is another important tip for you, if and when you decide to reach out to a counselor. Don't let a lack of funds stop you. Ask questions, do your research, get clear about possible insurance coverage or sliding scales. Find the right person at a rate you can handle. It might take a while, but it's totally worth it.

I found an affordable counselor and got to work on taking all that scary stuff out of my closet. I focused on my memories of being sexually abused.

Right away, I found a big difference between what I could remember about my experiences with my sister and what I could recall about my cousin. I shared all the details of Sarah, starting with that first day with my peanut butter and milk and *Scooby Doo* and what was being done to me under my blankie in the "safety" of my bedroom. We slowed it all down, took it apart. I told him all about the pain, the confusion, the fear, the shame I carried because she was a girl and around my age. Everything.

And just as that first counselor had explained, the abuse I suffered at the hands of my sister became a little less dark and scary. It was especially helpful that my counselor never suggested that a male can't be abused by a female, or that the abuser has to be x number of years older to be considered "real" abuse. He validated my experience all the way. That's one of the biggest gifts you can receive from counseling: having your experience and your feelings validated.

When it came to reaching into the closet and pulling out the scary part about the sexual abuse with my older cousin, however, the detailed memories just weren't there. I was so young when it happened that I could only recall general stuff: I picked him to be my babysitter. He made me do things I didn't want to do. Things like that. It was a start.

> **Healing Trauma Reminder: It's okay not to remember everything that happened to you; you work with whatever memories you do have.**

During the two years that I saw this counselor, I learned that you really don't have to remember it all to begin the process of getting better. You start with what you know, what you can remember. In time, more memories may come. Even if they don't, just sharing pieces of your experience and how it has affected you can be helpful.

Of course, I could get impatient at times. I wanted everything to get better quickly. When I discovered that my cousin Jimmy, my abuser, was dating someone with young children, I felt a gut instinct: *I've got to protect those kids!*

## Biblical Insight:

## A biblical example of following good counsel

Moses, who is considered one of the greatest men of the Bible, listened to good counsel and reaped the benefits of it.

## Story:

### Exodus 18:13-26 TLB

*The next day Moses sat as usual to hear the people's complaints against each other, from morning to evening. When Moses' father-in-law saw how much time this was taking, he said, "Why are you trying to do all this alone, with people standing here all day long to get your help?"*

*"Well, because the people come to me with their disputes, to ask for God's decisions," Moses told him. "I am their judge, deciding who is right and who is wrong, and instructing them in God's ways. I apply the laws of God to their particular disputes."*

*"It's not right!" his father-in-law exclaimed. "You're going to wear yourself out—and if you do, what will happen to the people? Moses, this job is too heavy a burden for you to try to handle all by yourself. Now listen, and let me give you a word of advice, and God will bless you: Be these people's lawyers—their representative before God—bringing him their questions to decide; you will tell them his decisions, teaching them God's laws, and showing them the principles of godly living.*

*"Find some capable, godly, honest men who hate bribes, and appoint them as judges, one judge for each 1000 people; he in turn will have ten judges under him, each in charge of a hundred; and under each of them will be two judges, each responsible for the affairs of fifty people; and each of these will have five judges beneath him, each counseling ten persons. Let these men be responsible to serve the people with justice at all times. Anything that is too important or complicated can be brought to you. But the smaller matters they can take care of themselves. That way it will be easier for you because you will share the burden with them. If you follow this advice, and if the Lord agrees, you will be able to endure the pressures, and there will be peace and harmony in the camp."*

*Moses listened to his father-in-law's advice and followed this suggestion. He chose able men from all over Israel and made them judges over the people—thousands, hundreds, fifties, and tens. They were constantly available to administer justice. They brought the hard cases to Moses but judged the smaller matters themselves.*

Confronting Your Perpetrator

**Scripture:**

**Romans 12:19 ESV**

***Beloved, never avenge yourselves but leave it to the wrath of God, for it is written, "'Vengeance is mine I will repay,' says The Lord."***

I made up my mind that I would track my cousin down, look him in the eye, and tell him that I know he abused me, that it was wrong, and that he had destroyed my childhood. I figured that would stop him from abusing those kids, while it would also wipe away the powerlessness that I always felt being around him ever since those horrifying days and nights when I was just a kid.

I had come face to face with my cousin one time, many years earlier, when he showed up at a playground across the street from our house. As soon as I spotted him, I ran, but Jimmy quickly tracked me down. Pulling me close that day long ago, he leaned toward me in that same terrifying way he used to do during that summer of hell, and he spoke the same words he had repeated over and over back then:

> *If you tell anybody what happened, I will kill you.*
> *Nobody would believe you anyway because you don't*
> *matter!*

Now, as an adult, I was going to confront my cousin about those words, about his abuse, about everything.

My counselor advised me about the dangers of confronting my abuser. He educated me about how abusers being confronted almost never admit to what happened. They usually deny, minimalize or distort the truth. Don't expect an apology. He also cautioned me that any encounter with my cousin could be very intense, that I could end up feeling re-traumatized by his negative or hostile reaction. I listened, but I wasn't convinced to give up my plan.

"Well, if you do choose to see him, I would strongly recommend that you don't go alone. Bring a friend with you," my counselor advised. "And if you're walking up to the place where you're going to see him and you get scared, don't go in. If you do go inside and you get scared waiting to confront him, leave."

I agreed to this plan and chose a friend from my recovery group to come with me. I was ready. Or so I thought.

My cousin was working at an upscale restaurant, with lots of wood and fancy wines. Not my kind of place at that time, but I was going to make it mine for this mission.

When my friend and I were approaching the entrance to the restaurant, I spotted Jimmy through a window. He spotted me, too. Immediately, he tried to stare me down. Suddenly, I felt that same kind of terror that haunted me when I was seven years old. For an instant, I considered running away, but something told me to keep walking. I managed to get inside and follow the host to our table. I kept reminding myself that I wasn't a skinny little kid anymore, I was 6-3, solidly built, only a few years removed from playing college basketball. I could do this.

Our server was taking our order when Jimmy walked by. He locked into me, giving me that look like he was going to hurt me. But instead of cowering, I gave him my best Mr. T look back. It was the first time that I had looked my abuser directly in the eye.

Unfortunately, that didn't stop my nerves from going absolutely berserk while we waited for our dinner. I had to go to the bathroom, like right away, and when I asked my friend to go with me because I was scared, he said, "No way. Women go to the bathroom together. We're guys." Not what I wanted and needed to hear from my ally during my confrontation.

In the bathroom, alone, I began to panic. The bathroom door did not have a lock and even after all those years, I still felt like I needed to be in a room with a door that closed and locked to feel safe and protected. *My cousin's going to come barging into this bathroom and hurt me, maybe even try to kill me!*

I finished doing my business as fast as I could, rushed back to the table, threw some money down to cover the bill, and bolted outside. The truth was that at that early stage of my healing, before I had even uncovered the vivid memories of the horrors I had lived through with my cousin, I really wasn't ready for confrontation. Just as my counselor warned me, I had been re-traumatized.

> **Insight for Loved Ones: If your loved one was abused by a family member, avoid pressuring him to engage with that perpetrating family member. Understand that it's empowering for him to say "no" when he was not allowed to say no before.**

### Breaking Free by Letting Go

What happened to me in the following days and weeks happens at some time to many men who commit to healing from trauma. They find that the process doesn't follow a neat, straight line, where things just keep getting easier and easier and life keeps getting better and better. Sometimes you have to plunge down into the darkness for a while before you can come back up into the light. And when that ride into the darkness comes, you just have to let go and ask for a lot of help and support. It's no time to go it alone.

Okay, I need to back up and give you some background here. I've got to explain how my abbreviated confrontation with my cousin, my abuser, was part of a perfect storm of events that threw me into a crisis. First, I was working full-time back then. Since I had embraced Christianity, I had realized that I couldn't continue my work as a DJ because of the inappropriate song lyrics and the whole unhealthy club scene. I turned to more of a regular job at an insurance agent's call center, while I was also going to school full- time at night to complete my college degree. Keeping up with that pace often left me worn out and frazzled.

At the same time, I was going through my painful divorce. That put a further strain on me physically, emotionally and financially. On top of all that, I had just come from a disturbing experience with my parents. I had recently begun to share bits and pieces with them about my counseling and my recovery work. My mom could hardly deal with it, other than to tell me she felt guilty that she didn't protect me. My dad's response was, well, not exactly what I would have hoped to receive. It came to a head during one visit when I told him it was time for me to go and he asked me where I was off to.

"A 12-Step meeting," I replied, truthfully.

My dad questioned why I had to go to these meetings, why I couldn't just suck it up. The whole manning up thing.

"I can't understand why you can't just get over that little abuse thing," he said.

*Little abuse thing?* Those years of living through sexual and physical abuse as a child, enduring the horrors and the shame, that all amounted to that *little abuse thing?* The huge meteor hit that left a crater in my life for years?

I usually treated my dad with a great deal of respect, but on that day I responded in a way that I never had before. I told him he had no idea what he was talking about, that he didn't understand the depth of pain I had experienced, and that I was not going to be judged by him.

I said what I needed to say, but the experience left me shaken and vulnerable. I was carrying that vulnerability when I tried to confront my cousin but wound up running away before I even tried to talk to him. And then I wound up re-living the trauma from my abuse.

The reignited trauma came out in a strange way. Not long after that moment with my cousin, I suddenly started flailing both my arms in front of my chest, a gesture that I couldn't control or stop. My counselor told me this was my body's way of remembering the sexual abuse with my cousin, an instinctive act of trying to push my abuser and everything about that awful experience away. He advised me that I was having a nervous breakdown and should check myself into a hospital.

Well, I didn't have the money or the insurance to cover some big hospital bill, so I vetoed that idea. What happened next was all about letting go, opening myself up to receiving help from many people, and trusting that I would get through to the other side of all this.

Here's what I later journaled about as I reflected on this very dark but very healing part of my life:

*The depth of my pain is nearly unbearable. But rather than stopping to process that pain, I have instead delved head first into work, going on months' long 70-to-100 hours a week work binges. A perfect storm of long hours and combination of events has finally taken me beyond my breaking point.*

*I'm in the middle of a very messy divorce, I just got criticized by my dad for going to counseling over what my dad called "that little sexual abuse thing" and he told me that I didn't need to grieve, that I should just suck it up and move on.*

*My business ventures are failing and for the first time in almost twenty years, I just ran into the male babysitter that abused me repeatedly for an entire summer when I was seven.*

*My entire being buckled under the weight of the burdens I'd carried for so long, and at age twenty-seven, I've just had a nervous breakdown. I can't work, can't function or care for myself at all. My mom had to fly in from across the country just to help take care of me. I am at the bottom. I am losing my businesses, losing my marriage, as well as losing the ability to have a daily relationship with my daughter.*

*I am sitting in a corner, unable to control my arms that are doing the same gestures uncontrollably, over and over again for days. Those gestures turned out to be my body remembering my severe and prolonged sexual abuse experiences. The gestures were of me repeatedly pushing the perpetrators away. My body was remembering what my memory for years did not. The abuse wasn't something I wanted, it wasn't something I deserved, it was something I tried to repel.*

In the midst of my deep and dark struggle, my pastor Ted told me that I should see Theo, a trusted mentor in the East Hill healing and recovery community. I agreed right away. Before our first session, I said yes to other unexpected help. My longtime friend

Jasmin told me I should not be living alone while I was going through this crisis. She personally reached out to my mom to ask her to come stay with me. By then, my parents had moved to Alaska where my dad had obtained a job on an oil platform. When my mom arrived, she jumped right in to fix my meals and do my chores while I focused on the bigger picture. Later, I even went to stay with my mom and dad in Alaska for a much-needed break from worries and responsibilities at home.

**Scripture:**

**Proverbs 19:20 ESV**

*Listen to advice and accept instruction, so that you may gain wisdom in the future.*

> **Insight for Loved Ones: When we're going through the darkest of times, taking time to help us with our basic needs, or just stopping by to check in on us, is invaluable. It gives us space to face our hurt.**

When I met with Theo, we agreed that I needed to focus on my sexual abuse history with my cousin. "But I still don't remember much," I said.

That's when Theo introduced me to another therapeutic tool. He called it "Pictures on the Wall." Here's how I understood it: when bad or good things happen in our lives, we take a picture of them in our minds. Sort of like how we link certain songs to specific experiences.

After Theo invited us to pray together, he asked me what picture was in my mind right then. It happened to be something related to my divorce proceedings. We looked at that picture briefly and then he asked me for the next picture that came to my mind, and the next one after that. Over a period of a few meetings, I had gone all the way back to that summer—the traumatic period of sexual abuse with my cousin.

"But there's a curtain right in front of those pictures," I said. "I'm too scared to look at what's behind that curtain."

"I understand," Theo said. "I have an idea. I'm going to pray that if you are meant to remember those things behind the curtain, God will help you remember them. Whenever that happens, we will meet and look at them together. Does that sound oaky?"

I agreed. I was willing to do anything that might help me get through this nervous breakdown or healing crisis or whatever anyone called it. When I got home, I sat down to pray:

> *God, I just want to get better. I don't know what it will take to get me better or how much more of this I can take. But if remembering what happened to me when I was a child will help me get better, I am open to that remembering. I pray for your help and your guidance.*

I went to bed feeling peaceful for the first time in weeks. When I woke up, I reached for a pad of paper by my bedside and began to write. I was filled with memory after memory of my sexual abuse with my cousin. I wrote and I wrote and didn't stop until I had filled up fifteen pages!

I called Theo, and we began working through those memories and the feelings that went with them. Talk about "going there!" I had opened a new door to my recovery and healing. It was a huge step in getting my life back.

Theo was a rock in steering me through the process. I remember a couple of key messages he conveyed to me:

"You are very brave to share these memories and face what happened to you."

"You didn't do anything wrong."

I really got it: I didn't do anything wrong. That's why in all the years since then, it has been easy and natural for me to publicly share the story of my abuse. It doesn't say anything about me or anything I did, it says things about *him*.

> **Healing Trauma Reminder: If you were abused, it's important to remember that you didn't do anything wrong.**

Now I don't want to give the impression that after I made it through my nervous breakdown, everything was easy, upbeat, happy-face wonderful. No, it was a slow path. I would continue to face more challenges and be called on to do a lot more of this kind of healing work in my commitment to keep getting better, which I'll share more about in the next couple of chapters.

## "Going There" Takes You to a Healthier Place

I had always feared hitting a bottom point in my life. Well, I sure hit it! But I discovered that in going there, I was not alone. I had help from people and forces that I never imagined would step up for me. And I came through it all in a much stronger, healthier place.

So, when you begin to "go there" and commit to your own healing path, wherever it leads you, I'm here to assure you that you can come through it all in a better place, too. And that's something that you, and any man who has survived trauma, absolutely deserves.

**Scripture:**

**Psalm 107: 1-9 MSG**

*Oh, thank God—He's so good!*

*His love never runs out.*

*All of you set free by God, tell the world!*

*Tell how He freed you from oppression,*

*Then rounded you up from all over the place,*

*from the four winds, from the seven seas.*

*Some of you wandered for years in the desert,*

*looking but not finding a good place to live,*

*Half-starved and parched with thirst,*

*staggering and stumbling, on the brink of exhaustion.*

*Then, in your desperate condition, you called out to God.*

*He got you out in the nick of time;*

*He put your feet on a wonderful road*

*that took you straight to a good place to live.*

*So thank God for His marvelous love,*

*For His miracle mercy to the children He loves.*

*He poured great drafts of water down parched throats;*

*the starved and hungry got plenty to eat.*

**Scripture:**

**Psalm 103:6 ESV**

*The Lord works righteousness and justice for all who are oppressed.*

**Prayer:**

Father,

Your word says that where there is no guidance, I will fall. Bring into my life godly counselors who are excellent followers of Jesus. With these godly counselors, I will ensure my safety. In Jesus' name,

Amen.

# 10

## BREAKING FREE FROM THE SHACKLES

### BY FOLLOWING THE HEALING PATH

> *Healing is not a one-time event but rather a journey. It's a process of going from point A to B and takes time, energy, and commitment."*
>
> - Jasmin Lee Cori, MS, LPC, *Healing from Trauma*

As men, we like to get clear on the goal or objective in front of us and act swiftly to fulfill it. If we're going to the store, we take a detailed list of what we need, find the items as fast as we can, march to checkout to pay and get out. If something breaks at home, we figure out the problem and fix it without a fuss or bother. If we get sick, we want a quick diagnosis, we take the medicine we're directed to use, and we get back to work. Boom, boom, boom.

It's not surprising, then, that when I'm helping men take their first steps in healing from trauma or helping them move on to the next step in their healing journey, they want the process to follow that same boom-boom-boom rhythm. They seek immediate results, a rapid march to the finish line. They figure that any and all kinds of mental, emotional, psychological and spiritual damage their trauma may have caused will just get fixed up in a jiffy and sent packing. They'll be all healed up and ready to go skating along in life.

That's when I have to bring in this little reality message: Not. So. Fast.

## Healing Is Not a Quick-Fix

**Scripture:**

**Galatians 6:9 ESV**

*And let us now grow weary of doing good, for in due season we will reap, if we do not give up.*

Hey, I'm all about finding any possible way to break free from the shackles caused by trauma. Free to have more great things in life and to get rid of the crappy things. Free to experience more peace, satisfaction, happiness, pleasure. Free to build and sustain healthy and meaningful relationships, to pursue work with meaning and purpose, to seek and follow our personal connection with God. Free to wake up in the morning without the burden of shame. Free of the weight of painful memories that hold us back or pull us down.

But here's the thing about how we break free from those shackles and become free, unbound. It's not a one-shot deal. We don't break free in one big burst. It's more like we enter into an ongoing commitment to keep breaking free from the shackles. We don't show up at some one-stop big box Therapy Store, grab a couple of items to check off our list and come out all healed. It's more like we follow an ongoing, full-time path of healing.

Bear with me while I try to explain this in a different way. As I tell many of the men that I help, when you're trying to get better after surviving some kind of trauma, it's more useful to set your goals around "healing", in that "ing" form of the word, than it is to aim for being "healed," or the "ed" form of the word.

What does that mean? Well, for most of us, the expectation we carry fits that "ed" version, meaning that we assume that in a very short time, with minimal effort and action on our part, we're just going to get all fixed up, all healed. We'll be good to go. The truth is that healing usually happens in that "ing" version, not the "ed" form. The process you're committing to is about "healing," not "getting healed."

Even though we might want it to be different, healing from trauma is an ongoing process. That's why we take it slow, and why we celebrate our progress. The thing is, if we think about the process as being all about getting "healed," that mindset feeds into a performance treadmill that can leave us more wounded when we don't reach that "ed" state in the manner or speed we want or expect.

Okay, that's enough of my little "ing" vs. "ed" explanation. Don't worry if you're not sure you would pass the test on my little lesson!

**Insight for Loved Ones: Expecting him to get better right away will create frustration for you and shame for him. Be flexible enough to adjust your own expectations about how rapidly his healing will progress.**

What else does it help to know about following the healing path? It's a path on which we may be called upon at any time to climb high peaks or descend into low valleys. And follow a whole bunch of twists and turns. And learn to read new signs and navigate rapidly shifting terrain. Each and every new step we take will, hopefully, bring us toward something better in our lives. But we've still got to keep taking that next step.

**Scripture:**

**1 Corinthians 15:58 NLT**

*Therefore, my beloved brothers, be steadfast, immovable, always abounding in the work of the Lord, knowing that in the Lord your labor is not in vain.*

As you travel down this healing path, here are two important reminders that will help keep you on track:

- Give yourself credit for any progress you are making at every step along the way.
- Keep taking advantage of new opportunities for healing that show up on your path.

I'll give you a real-life example to give you a better idea of following this healing path. It's about a friend from one of my addiction recovery groups. While I was managing to stay sober in my addiction to porn, Lucas was stumbling, with relapses every month or so.

"I'm really frustrated," Lucas told me.

"I understand," I said, "but you know what? Your life *is* getting better." Lucas looked at me a little funny and asked me what I meant by that.

"Think about it big-picture here," I urged. "You used to turn to porn every day, right? Well, now you use porn once a month. So, in a year with 365 days, you are sober for 353 days. It's only the other twelve days when you're not sober. You and I know the goal is to stay sober all the time, and I support you in that because we all know that there are true benefits to continuous sobriety. But think about how far you've come from where you were. You're still moving toward recovery. You're still following a path of healing."

Others may disagree, but I believe that when we're trying to heal from trauma, any and all signs of progress are important and worth acknowledging. Perfection is not the goal here. There is a 12-Step saying that really applies here: "progress not perfection."

Let's say you used to yell at your partner once a week and now you yell at them once a month. And when it happens now, you're much more aware of what you're doing and why, you try to make things right with her immediately, and you call upon the tools you've been learning to continue to curb your expressions of anger or disrespect. To me, that's part of the process of breaking free from the shackles. You're moving the needle toward healing.

I've seen how this works time and time again on my journey toward healing. Right after my nervous breakdown, I finally admitted to myself that I had an eating problem. In the midst of that stormy period triggered by going off to confront my cousin about being sexually abused, I had gained thirty or forty pounds. Late at night, I'd devour donuts and cake, consume entire half gallons of ice cream, usually smothered with hot fudge sauce, and I still had a sweet spot for big jars of peanut butter that I'd eat in large quantities with a spoon.

I could have just ignored this "little" problem with my eating habits, but by then I knew that if I was serious about following a path of healing, I couldn't overlook new stuff that came along that needed my attention. I looked up the 12-Step resources for Overeaters Anonymous and began attending those meetings, while still keeping up with my other recovery work.

**Healing Trauma Reminder: When a new symptom of trauma shows up, remember to call upon any resources that you have already benefitted from to help address the problem.**

After acknowledging this new addiction, I was urged to identify one part of my eating routine to let go of. I chose to stop eating cake with my ice cream. Yeah, I was still eating my ice cream but at least I wasn't using that as an excuse to chow down big pieces of cake. When I was successful in achieving that goal, I gave myself credit, then set out to take the next step in my recovery. I also worked on identifying what I ate and what I was feeling when I ate it.

Soon, I recognized that over-eating was one more symptom of my sexual trauma. How? Because I would eat to try to numb myself so I wouldn't have to be swallowed up by the intense shame, fear and battered self-esteem I still carried from being abused. Little by little, I have moved toward releasing myself from the shackles of my eating addiction.

Making the commitment to pursue healing on this new front also opened doors in other important areas. Most of the attendees of these Overeaters Anonymous meetings were women. One of these women, Toni, became my sponsor. As I got to know her, I learned that she was pursuing a goal to become a massage therapist and was looking for people to practice massage on. "Hey, maybe we can help each other here," I suggested.

I explained my sexual abuse history with both a male and a female perpetrator, and I told her that I needed to learn how to receive and experience healthy non-sexual touch. I had never even had a massage before, and I figured this would be a good way to start.

Toni agreed to this plan, and she made things easy for me with her caring, motherly presence. She started slowly, allowing me to wear big baggy shorts during the first couple of massages. Gradually, I got comfortable with receiving pleasurable touch on my body that was not sexual. This was a big gift for me in my healing from abuse.

## A Taste of Healing

As men who have survived trauma, we each have our own experience when we follow the healing path. Whatever approach you take to get better, and no matter what resources you call upon, don't get discouraged when it doesn't happen all at once. Celebrate those small steps marking your progress. And when you're focusing on one particular trauma or symptom of trauma, don't close yourself off to opportunities to take a step forward somewhere else.

Here's my attitude toward getting better: if I tasted a little bit of healing, I would say to myself, "I've got to have more of this!" I was so tired of being in pain from all my childhood trauma, I just felt wide open to anything that might help. I figured that if I'm paying a therapist $100 an hour and he tells me to go read a book that could help me, I'm going right out to buy that book and read it cover to cover. I'd be wasting my time and money if I didn't.

Don't worry if you're not quite so gung-ho about diving into each and every available healing opportunity that pops up in front of you. Go at your own pace, choose what feels right to you, and remember that what's really important is what you get out of every stop along your journey.

It's true that recovery and healing can be hard at times, but the pain and the shame you live with if you don't commit to the healing path is much harder. When I was suffering from all the crap I had been through, I really did have that feeling of being shackled or chained by something. Each time I made progress in my healing, I felt that I was doing something to help me break free from those shackles. But sometimes it just seemed like I would break from the shackles binding my hands and arms, only to find that I was still shackled by some other pain that was chaining down my legs and my feet.

**Biblical Insight:**

**A biblical example of how healing is a process**

There is a unique story in the Bible of a man who was eventually healed from blindness in Matthew, Chapter 8. Four distinct steps took place in this healing process. First, Jesus removed the man away from the people who brought him. Second, Jesus smeared spit on his eyes, but all the man could see was the movement of chunky tree-like figures. And then Jesus laid hands on him again and this time, he was able to see clearly! Finally, Jesus directed him not to return to the village where he lived.

Healing can be a process. There were other factors at work in this man's life that had to be addressed. Jesus took the time needed and worked with the man, helping him to receive his complete healing.

**Story:**

**Mark 8:22-26 GNT**

*They came to Bethsaida, where some people brought a blind man to Jesus and begged Him to touch him. Jesus took the blind man by the hand and led him out of the village. After spitting on the man's eyes, Jesus placed His hands on him and asked him, "Can you see anything?"*

*The man looked up and said, "Yes, I can see people, but they look like trees walking around."*

*Jesus again placed His hands on the man's eyes. This time the man looked intently, his eyesight returned, and he saw everything clearly. Jesus then sent him home with the order, "Don't go back into the village."*

> **Healing Trauma Reminder: Healing can be hard, but the pain from not healing is much harder.**

All the while that I was looking out for new resources to help me get better, I still had some feeling, a deep-in-my-soul belief that my life had a greater purpose beyond all my struggles and setbacks. I had a sense that I could someday give other people some kind of lift while they tried to heal from their own pain. And I knew that if I was ever going to step into that role, I would have to stay on that healing path I had started on.

**Scripture:**

**Romans 8:28 NLT**

*And we know that God causes everything to work together for the good of those who love God and are called according to His purpose for them.*

## A Relationship That Actually Gets Better!

A big part of breaking free was figuring out how to have a healthy relationship. That sure wasn't happening during my Romeo years of sexual conquest, and my attempt to build a marriage with the mother of my daughter had totally failed. In the fallout from that breakup, I got hit by a bunch of zings and arrows that just kept knocking me further into the pit.

When I remember those days, I feel deep gratitude for my pastor, Ted. He stood right beside me through my long, draining divorce, especially near the end when I was tempted to rise up off the turf and keep fighting.

"Our God is big," Ted said. "God will redeem this. Just let it go."

And that's just what I did. Not only did I let go of all the conflict tangled up in the divorce process, I also buckled down to making myself a healthier person before I could even attempt to enter into a healthy relationship. Believe it or not, this guy who used to bounce from one-night stand to one-night stand spent the next five years single and celibate. That's the period when I was focusing on my relationship with God while pursuing counseling to address my sexual trauma and other traumas, and I attended every group that could contribute some new piece to my healing.

Since I was divorced, I figured I could benefit from taking a divorce recovery class. I found it very helpful in understanding my mistakes and my habits in relationships, and I gained a different point of view from the women in the group. Many of them were much healthier emotionally than all the women I had known.

Another experience opened my eyes about how I could approach women and sex much differently than I had been doing. My mom and dad were living a short distance from me at the time, and a young woman living across the street from them began showing up at their doorstep with black eyes and a disheveled appearance. The guy Sandy was living with was beating her. She would rush over to their house when he wasn't home, hoping that she might find temporary safety or a sympathetic ear. My parents tried to offer that to her.

Sandy happened to show up once or twice while I was visiting my mom and dad, and then one day she knocked on their door while I was there and my parents were out. She was a mess, and I knew that jerk had hit her again. I thought maybe I could help by taking her away from the scene and getting her something to eat, so I invited her to my place.

"I'm really sorry that this guy is treating you so badly," I said as I fixed her coffee and scrounged around my kitchen to put together a few groceries for her to take home. "No one should ever be afraid of getting hit by their partner. I hope you can find a way out of this situation."

Meanwhile, I couldn't help noticing that Sandy was an extremely attractive woman. Yeah, my body was going berserk. But I didn't act on that impulse. "Do not take advantage of this human being," I said to myself. I had to repeat those words a few times before getting calm enough to drive her home and wish her well.

A week or two later, Sandy showed up at my doorstep. After I invited her in, she blurted out, "Nobody has ever treated me the way you treated me the other day! You were so kind and I . . . well, I just really wanted to thank you, to show my appreciation." Well, I was a guy, and I had been around long enough to get the idea.

"Listen, I think you're a really beautiful woman," I said. "But I'm still married (my divorce was not yet final at the time) and I'm a Christian. I really appreciate you wanting to say thank-you to me, and I'm not rejecting you, but . . . well, I just value you too much to go any further."

Sandy looked shocked, and I had surprised myself that I could deal with temptation in this way. It was one more example of how being on the healing path leads to changes in your behavior and your thinking. I recognized that what this woman was willing to give me was not what I needed to heal. What I did next was an even stronger symbol of the new Matt.

"Before you go, I just want to tell you about this class I've been going to at my church," I said. "It's for adult children of dysfunctional families and how our lives get messed up by things that have happened to us when we were growing up. I don't really know you that well, but I just thought this was something that you might find helpful." I handed her the manual for the class and told her to keep it—even if she wasn't able to make the class, maybe it could help her.

She politely thanked me and soon headed home, no doubt still shocked at having a man choose not to come on to her after she had so obviously opened the door. I figured that would be the last I would see of Sandy.

Two years later, I was in church one Sunday when I happened to turn around and notice a strikingly beautiful woman. Sandy looked different: nicer clothes, makeup, hair, nails—all put together. It was clear that she was no longer being battered and that something good was happening in her life.

"I'm glad I found you here, Matt," she said. "I've been hoping that I would have the chance to tell you how much it meant to me that you treated me that way. You helped me realize that I had value. I left that guy soon after that. I've got a good job. Things are coming together for me. Oh, and that class you mentioned to me that day, I checked it out and have been going to it for over a year. It's really helped me."

"You're welcome," was all I could say as I smiled.

Sometime after this experience, I finally felt like I was ready to start dating again. It had been five years of focusing only on my recovery and my healing. Now it was time to explore how I could share my "healing life" with someone else.

I met Laura at church when we were both participating in East Hill's Valentine's Day program. I was part of a Christian rap performance. In a separate act, Laura sang the Carole King song *I Feel the Earth Move*. As I watched her and listened to her, things started moving inside me, too. One day a group of us went out to eat together after church, and Laura wound up in the front seat of my Jeep. We started to talk and right away I was saying to myself:

"Wow! She's so authentic, so open, so direct, so deep. No games, nothing. She's just real!"

We started dating and telling stories about our lives. It turned that we both had survived major trauma. I won't go into details about Laura's past—that's something that she gets to choose if and when to share with others. I'll just say that in addition to being an incredible singer, I soon learned that Laura was one very strong woman. As we drew closer, it blew me away to find myself in my first relationship where the longer we were together, the better our relationship just kept getting.

**Healing Trauma Reminder: If you wait until you have done a lot of healing from your trauma, you'll have a much better chance of building a successful relationship.**

We got married on May 1$^{st}$, choosing that date because it was the anniversary of my first day going to 12-Step meetings several years earlier. Like most couples, we've had our challenges over the last twenty-plus years, but we've held solidly to our commitment to one another, and to keep following our own healing paths.

If you had told me twenty-five years ago that I could ever make that statement about a relationship with a woman in my life, I would have said "no way!" But that's what can happen when you choose to keep following the healing path. Good things happen to you, things that you never thought would show up on the video highlights of your life. The possibilities just keep growing and expanding.

**Scripture:**

**Lamentations 3:25 ESV**

***The Lord is good to those who wait for Him, to the soul who seeks Him.***

## As You Heal, You Just Get Bigger

Sometimes you may notice signs of how you're getting bigger as a person. I had an experience of how this works while waiting in line at Pepino's, a popular Portland restaurant a few blocks from one of the largest centers for 12-Step meetings in the city. I would often go there before or after meetings. People waiting in the long line to get into the restaurant would often get aggressive, and I would usually let people cut in on me or push me around. One day this guy stepped in front of me, just like it had happened what seemed like a hundred times before that. Only this time, I reacted differently.

I just looked at that line-cutter for a moment. Then I said, "Excuse me, man, but I'm in line here. I've been waiting a long time, and I'm not going to wait longer because of you. You need to get behind me." At first, he gave me that look, like he was expecting me to feel intimidated and back down. But I didn't back down, and a few seconds later he quietly stepped in line behind me.

**Scripture:**

**2 Timothy 1:7 NLT**

*For God has not given us a spirit of fear and timidity, but of power, love, and self-discipline.*

This little gesture gave me more evidence of how I really was getting better in my healing from trauma. I had stood up for myself and proved that I was not at the whim of what anybody wanted to do to me at any time they wanted to do it.

In sexual abuse recovery, there's a term for how this works. It's called "Bigefy." I learned this tool at a recovery conference, and it was first developed by Dr. Paul Linden, a psychologist. The way I understand it, we sexual abuse survivors tend to get small, physically and emotionally, any time we feel at all threatened or under attack. We retreat and protect ourselves; we actually "smallify." This is especially true when we're dealing with the people closest to us emotionally, but it can show up at other times too.

In my situation, I became aware of how I would often keep my hands on my lap, or actually a little lower, like I was trying to protect my private parts. This kind of posture, a remnant of my sexual abuse, sure didn't put me in a position to deal with emotionally charged situations in a way that allowed me to say what I needed to say and ask for and receive what I needed. To change this pattern, I had to learn to "bigefy." Here's how it works, as I interpreted it:

Instead of collapsing our bodies, we open up our arms wide, take deep breaths, relax our shoulders and our belly and visualize something/someone that makes us feel happy and loved. This puts us in a position of power and compassion and makes us better equipped to deal with challenging people and situations in a stronger, more adult way.

This is just one of a whole bunch of tools and techniques that I have learned and practiced in following my healing path. (I will provide a list of many of these tools at the end of this book.) When I was trying to pave the way for a healthy relationship and keep building on what Laura and I were creating together, it really helped me to learn about a popular psychological model called attachment theory. Basically, our attachment style is how we approach our most important relationships, and it usually comes from influences and experiences from when we were growing up.

As a sexual abuse survivor, I had developed an attachment style where I would always worry about whether I could be loved, leaving me needing validation or approval. It led me to approach my relationships with weak boundaries and to try to manipulate the other person. I needed to become confident that I really was worthy of love. I had to learn to be able to trust so I wouldn't act in stupid ways that would make it hard for me to get what I wanted and needed.

> **Healing Trauma Reminder: When you believe that you are really worthy of love, you are in a much better position to receive it.**

Okay, I admit that this is one of those changes that can really take time, effort and patience. But when you stick with the idea that you're on a healing path, you understand that. And you take time to give yourself credit when you make any small step in the new direction you're aiming to follow. Then you open your eyes to new ways to get better.

**Scripture:**

**Philippians 4:6 MSG**

*Don't fret or worry. Instead of worrying, pray. Let petitions and praises shape your worries into prayers, letting God know your concern.*

After several years of benefitting from 12-Step recovery work for addiction to porn and overeating, I identified a third addiction. After I got married and Laura and I started a family (our two sons plus my daughter), I noticed how I would often check out of family activities by consuming myself in my work. I was always trying to run some new business, which meant eighty-hour work weeks, and when we sat down to watch a movie together, I'd be glued to my laptop. I was disconnecting from those I wanted to be the closest to. I was showing signs of Workaholism.

Instead of denying that this problem was real, or that it was important, I found a 12-Step meeting to address it. Making the commitment to Workaholics Anonymous became invaluable later in my life when work sucked up all my time and energy again.

## Ending the Generational Curse

**Scripture:**

**Exodus 34:6-7 GNT**

*"...I, the Lord, am a God who is full of compassion and pity, who is not easily angered and who shows great love and faithfulness. I keep my promise for thousands of generations and forgive evil and sin."*

Here's another way to validate yourself and what you're doing as you follow your own healing path. If you came from an upbringing where you were surrounded by painful, traumatic or dysfunctional influences, remind yourself that you are the dam trying to hold back all the stuff that happened in your family during your childhood. Even if some water seeps through now and again, you are determined to remain firm as that dam in place, without being blown over by the circumstances and situations in your life today. In other words, you're going to stop the flow of the generational trauma, dysfunction and pattern of keeping secrets that were handed down to you.

This reminder has worked very well for me. I've had so many times in my life when I have felt my parents' dysfunctional beliefs, or their parents' dysfunctional beliefs, to be present like poison in my body, and also in our entire family system. But as I continued to get better, I could see how their ways were not my ways. Little by little, I was building and maintaining this dam that would stop the influences from pouring over into my words, actions and beliefs.

## Women Are Vital to Helping Us Men Heal

As you follow the healing path, it can also help to remind yourself that as a guy, your approach to growth, change, recovery and healing is probably going to look different than it does for most women. Women who want us to change *today* easily and understandably can forget this!

When I am called on to talk to women whose male loved ones are trying to heal from trauma, I urge them not to expect too much too soon. As I mentioned earlier, it's really important to have realistic expectations, to give a guy space to do what he needs to do. Recovery and healing take time, and if you put pressure on him, or you want him to do it your way, you're going to make things harder for both of you. Understand that the process he's following is not about transformation, it's about healing.

**Insight for Loved Ones: The more patience you extend to him, the faster and more thoroughly he'll move through the healing process, and the more benefits you will receive from having a healthier male in your life.**

If you feel that you have a useful suggestion to offer, give him time to figure out if it's something that fits for him. If you can affirm the work he's doing, help him acknowledge the progress he's making, and assure him that you're committed to standing beside him through all the tough stuff on the healing path, you will be making a great contribution in his life.

We all need to recognize that there are often lots of differences in how guys take on their healing than how it may work for women. One difference that I often see is that men tend to deal with painful situations or try to take a step forward in their healing by *doing*. As an example, I remember a friend who told me that when he first learned that his dad had passed away, he went right out to chop some wood. In the midst of his sweating and pounding, he was releasing his feelings over this loss.

Lots of men will do the same kind of thing by playing golf, tennis or handball. The whole idea of doing all our healing work by sitting still in some counselor's office and trying to explain our feelings can sound terrifying. We may need to do that sometimes, as we have discussed, but we still may be looking to balance that kind of healing work with some kind of doing.

**Healing Trauma Reminder: Sometimes men are more comfortable healing by doing.**

At one of the healing conferences that I attended for sexual abuse survivors, I noticed that when guys were sharing their painful stories in front of a group of other men, they would often get up and start pacing as they spoke. Many guys find it almost impossible to just sit stoically around a table while they confide things that are both painful and vulnerable.

Today, when a man seeks me out looking for support or guidance to help him deal with the symptom of a major trauma, he's usually going to feel more willing to say what he needs to say while we're doing something together: having a cup of coffee, grabbing some lunch, working out at the gym, sitting in the steam room. It's just the way we're wired.

If you find that you're more comfortable dealing with your pain and struggles while mixing in some form of doing, I urge you to find ways to do so on your own and to let any professional caregiver assisting you know that this is something that you need. If it can help to show them this book and tell them Matt says it's important to make room for healing by doing, be my guest!

## Is There a List That Tells Me That I'm Getting Better?

Now, before we wrap up this chapter, I'm guessing that some of you may be saying, "I don't know how patient this guy expects me to be. I'm a man—I need some concrete signs that tell me that I'm really healing, that I'm fulfilling my mission here. Can you show me some sign that I'm headed in the right direction and making tangible progress?"

I don't think there's one sure-fire, set-in-stone signal that you've done it, that you've earned your degree in this "healing university" you've enrolled in. It's a journey, remember. But as a trauma survivor, I have seen a few lists of signposts and checkpoints that clinicians have put together to help us identify our progress in a way that enables us to see and acknowledge it. Let's take a composite look at what they say about pinpointing changes that show we're definitely healing, that we're making the kind of progress we really want to see:

- 1. The symptoms of your trauma have become something that you are better able to recognize, understand and at least manage in your day-to-day life.

- 2. You can tell the story about your trauma and how it impacted you with a sense of meaning and feeling, without getting overwhelmed by your emotions.

- 3. You have a better way of knowing what you are feeling, not only about your trauma but about things happening in your life in the here and now.

- 4. You're more confident in who you are and what you can do, and you're finding ways to ask for and receive what you need.

- 5. You are better able to approach your relationships as more of an adult, rather than a victim.

If you don't feel like you're anywhere close to scoring a good grade on these checkpoints, don't be discouraged. Even many years after I had set foot on my healing path, I sure wasn't getting all A's. Our changes tend to come in fits and starts.

In the next chapter, I'll share with you an experience I had when I found myself taking one bold, giant step forward on my healing journey. It was a leap that I never would have been able to make without my commitment to follow my healing path wherever it took me, for as long as it was going to take.

**<u>Prayer:</u>**

Father,

I trust You with all my heart. I will not lean on my own understanding but will obey Your word and follow my counselors' instructions.

When I'm weak and stumble, I will consider the progress I have made along the way and let it encourage me. I will not give up. I will continue to progress through each phase of healing, trusting that the outcome will be successful. In Jesus' name I pray,

Amen.

## 11

# BREAKING FREE FROM THE SHACKLES

### BY RELEASING OUR HEAVIEST BURDENS

*"Forgiveness is one way that all creatures can deal with those eventsthat wound the soul."*

- Everett L. Worthington Jr., *Forgiving and Reconciling: Bridges to Wholeness and Hope*

All along in this book, we've been talking about the many different kinds of trauma that men suffer. Trauma also comes in many different degrees. Author Maggie Scarf put a name to that when she explained that we can have "big-T traumas" or "little-t traumas."

The way I understand it, a little-t trauma might be something like getting rear-ended in a car accident and walking away without severe injuries. That accident may impact you, making you a little nervous whenever somebody starts pulling up close behind your car. But it's not likely to traumatize you to the point of giving you nightmares, dragging you down into addictions, messing up all your relationships or turning your whole life upside down.

A big-T trauma, on the other hand, is the kind of trauma we have mostly been talking about. Physical, sexual or emotional abuse. Major losses. A medical crisis. The biggest of the big-T traumas are the ones that dig in deep and keep showing up in your life, even after you believe you've been traveling down the healing path forever. And when they show up in ways you just can't tolerate anymore, you may find yourself going all-in on some bold, new approaches to getting better.

What I want to share with you now relates to the greatest tools and techniques that I've used to date. They produced large-scale transformational healing in my life. Here's the story:

About ten years ago, my stress level had gone shooting way up, mostly because for what seemed like the zillionth time in my life, my work and career path had gone off track. That triggered lots of anxiety in my marriage and family.

It's not like I had never tasted any kind of success. I was very popular in my DJ days until that kind of work no longer fit my Christian beliefs and my addiction recovery. Later, I helped put together an organization called Extraordinary Young People (EXYP). Basically, I combined my two loves of music and basketball to create a Christian-based hip-hop church and launch youth centers and other youth programs on Native American reservations. We were a big hit at the Crow Indian Reservation, near the site of the Battle of Little Bighorn, and the Warm Springs Reservation in Oregon. Unfortunately, funding issues got in the way and I had to go back to my pattern of hip-hopping across career tracks. I even dabbled in real estate, just in time to get derailed in the housing market crash.

During this particular period of high stress, Laura and I knew that our marriage needed help. We began seeing a counselor specializing in recovery from sexual abuse. Greg gave me one useful tool right off the bat. When Laura and I sat in counseling sessions together, he would ask me how I felt about something and I would say, "I have no clue. I still don't have a good sense of my feelings, except maybe anger. Oh, and I know when I'm feeling unsafe."

Greg introduced me to a tool that lists sixty-four emotions or feeling states in a way that helps you track what you are experiencing down to a root emotion. It's called The Feeling Wheel, and it was developed by Dr. Gloria Willcox, author of the book *Feelings: Converting Negatives to Positives.* Many clinicians, groups and organizations have called upon this tool to help men and women improve their understanding of their emotions. This tool seemed to revolutionize my awareness of my feelings overnight! For example, I learned that when I say "I'm tired" it could really mean "I'm sad." Anxiety could be traced to fear, or frustration to anger.

But Greg would bring much more to my healing table. Soon after he began seeing Laura and me together, he advised us to work with him separately. When Greg began zeroing in on my sexual abuse history, he noticed right away that my feelings toward my cousin were still, well, you might say *intense*. He made a suggestion.

"Matt, if you really want to get all this stuff out of you so it stops influencing your life, there's something I can teach you that's like an atomic bomb version of healing from this kind of abuse," Greg explained. "It can be really hard, but I know you are capable of doing the work."

Greg then explained a process that guides you through an experience of having a "conversation" with those who inflicted trauma in your life and then taking the further step of forgiving them.

Okay, you're probably reading those words and thinking, "Wait, what? I'm supposed to *forgive* that monster who abused me, that animal who tried to destroy my life? No way!"

I totally get that kind of response. So, before I even get into the details of how this process wound up giving me a big boost of momentum in my life, I need to say that when you're just stepping foot on the healing path after surviving major trauma like sexual abuse, this is probably not something you're going to want to take on. You might want to just file it away for future consideration, when you're working with a healing professional that you trust and you're open to something new and different because you really *really* want to let go of the heavy burdens you're still carrying.

As Greg explained it to me, this forgiveness process was something to help get me to the point where I could finally stop carrying the weight of my abusers on my shoulders. One way or another, that's what I had been doing for thirty years—way too long! That burden was still limiting what I could achieve in my life, sapping me of the strength to do what I was really capable of doing.

I also learned that this kind of forgiveness is not something you do for the other person. It's something you are totally doing for *you*. It's kind of like you make a decision not to be the judge anymore. That doesn't mean that you excuse what your abuser did. No way. When I set out to follow this process of forgiveness related to my cousin, I was very clear that what he did was . . . what he did.

But I realized that trying to be the judge all the time just kept me in prison. It's that thing about drinking poison over and over and expecting somebody else to die. I was actually giving power to my cousin, and this new process was one big way to take that power back.

I also liked the idea because my cousin was far and away the heaviest burden I was carrying. I was tired of picking him up all the time. I was really ready to release him in the form of releasing those burdens he had projected onto me.

## Biblical Insight:

### A biblical example of how forgiveness can be a weapon

Jesus gives us an object lesson in forgiveness. Forgiveness is a major weapon of righteousness that removes the mountains of challenges that we face, and it brings phenomenal answers to our prayers.

## Scripture:

### Mark 11: 12- 14,20-25 MSG

*As they left Bethany the next day, he was hungry. Off in the distance he saw a fig tree in full leaf. He came up to it expecting to find something for breakfast, but found nothing but fig leaves. (It wasn't yet the season for figs.) He addressed the tree: "No one is going to eat fruit from you again—ever!" And his disciples overheard him…*

*In the morning, walking along the road, they saw the fig tree, shriveled to a dry stick. Peter, remembering what had happened the previous day, said to him, "Rabbi, look—the fig tree you cursed is shriveled up!"*

*Jesus was matter-of-fact: "Embrace this God-life. Really embrace it, and nothing will be too much for you. This mountain, for instance: Just say, 'Go jump in the lake'—no shuffling or hemming and hawing—and it's as good as done. That's why I urge you to pray for absolutely everything, ranging from small to large. Include everything as you embrace this God-life, and you'll get God's everything. And when you assume the posture of prayer, remember that it's not all asking. If you have anything against someone, forgive—only then will your heavenly Father be inclined to also wipe your slate clean of sins."*

**Biblical Insight:**

Jesus teaches that if we cooperate with God and forgive the perpetrator who offended us, God is able to deal with their hearts and consciences in such an intense way, they will understand that God is real and that you belong to Him.

**Scripture:**

**Romans 12:16-19 TLB**

*Never pay back evil for evil. Do things in such a way that everyone can see you are honest clear through. Don't quarrel with anyone. Be at peace with everyone, just as much as possible.*

*Dear friends, never avenge yourselves. Leave that to God, for he has said that he will repay those who deserve it. Don't take the law into your own hands.*

**Biblical Insight:**

Jesus was the perfect role-model of forgiveness, and we should imitate Him.

**Scripture:**

**Luke 23:33-35 MSG**

*When they got to the place called Skull Hill, they crucified him, along with the criminals, one on his right, the other on his left.*

*Jesus prayed, "Father, forgive them; they don't know what they're doing."*

**1 Corinthians 11:1 TLB**

*And you should follow my example, just as I follow Christ's.*

> **Healing Trauma Reminder: Forgiving those who hurt you is not something you do for the other person, it's something you do for yourself.**

So I gave the green light to go forward with this process, which closely followed something called the REACH method outlined by

Everett L. Worthington Jr. in his excellent resource book *Forgiving and Reconciling*. I dove into it with the same commitment and focus I used to bring to my basketball game. An early step was to go home and think about questions Greg gave me about my sexual abuse with my cousin:

- What happened?

- How did I feel when it happened? How do I feel now writing about this?

- What did I wish I could have said or done to my cousin when I was being abused?

- What would I want to say to him now?

- How did the sexual abuse he inflicted on me affect me physically, emotionally, socially, spiritually?

## The Empty Chair

After that prep work, Greg led me into an exercise that I just thought of as "the empty chair." He brought out three chairs, and just the sight of those chairs jolted me—they were the same type of chairs as my dining room chairs at home! I was tempted to say something like, "Are you kidding me?" But I took a breath and let that go. Greg sat in one chair, I sat in another chair and the third chair was left empty.

For the first few minutes, I just talked about what I had written in answering those prep questions, and Greg asked me a few more. We had already spent time in earlier sessions processing some of the issues related to my sexual trauma with my cousin, so this wasn't unfamiliar ground. But what happened next was definitely new.

"So, when you are ready, close your eyes," Greg said. "Now this may feel a little unnatural at first because obviously your cousin is not here. But in a moment, we're going to imagine that you're inviting your cousin to sit in that empty chair." To invite my abuser into the room for real would have been super unsafe for me. But to pretend I was doing so, which allowed me to be safe and in control, that I was willing to do.

I nodded my head but kept my eyes closed. Greg asked me to imagine some of the things I remembered from that time and place. I had an image of a Miami Dolphins football helmet I kept in my bedroom when I was seven years old. I felt like I was right back there.

"Do you give permission for your cousin to walk in now and sit in that chair?" Greg asked. Surprisingly, I had no trouble granting my permission, because I was the one in control this time. My cousin couldn't hurt me.

"Yes, I give my permission," I said.

Slowly, Greg helped me imagine what was happening back then as if it were happening right here and now. I started to feel some of that same anger, hatred, fear. But this time, with my eyes now open, I had the chance to talk to my cousin as if he were there, instead of cowering in silence. I could use the words I had always been terrified to speak when he was abusing me and threatening me. Everything I couldn't or wouldn't dare to say then, I could say now.

I told my cousin just what he had done to me and how it had messed up my life. How he hurt me. Violated me. Made me do things I never wanted to do. How he terrified me, making me afraid to tell the truth or ask for help. How he ruined my childhood.

I told my cousin that it was never my fault, none of it, that it was all him. I let him know that what he did to me damaged my sexuality, leaving me with a pleasure-pain confusion and a big-time inability to trust. I went on to name the other negative ways he had influenced my whole life. I let him know very clearly that he was the one that started the fire that had been burning to some degree or other ever since.

I said it all and I said it crisp and clear, giving voice to what I had only indirectly said in counseling before. And when the process wound down, that heavy burden really did begin to lift from my shoulders.

"I Forgive You for . . ."

This atomic bomb version of healing wasn't over. After giving me time to relax from all the feelings stirred up from my experience with the empty chair, Greg guided me into the next step: writing a letter of forgiveness to my cousin. It would be a letter that I never intended to send to him, of course. This letter was for me, not him. It was another powerful way for me to really let go of all that anger, hatred, bitterness and resentment that had been dragging me down.

My letter started out with some of the same things I had said in the empty chair exercise, naming the things he had done to me and emphasizing that it was *not* my fault. But this time, I went on to a second part, beginning with the words "I forgive you for . . . " Then I made a list of all those ways my cousin had damaged my life. I was declaring that I was forgiving him for each of those horrific acts.

Was that hard to do? Brutally hard! But I stuck with it, experiencing many different feelings along the way. I was better able to identify those feelings by using the Feelings Wheel. As I chose to get in touch with my feelings and actually sit with them rather than avoiding them, it helped lift those burdens I had been carrying. As I often say, "You gotta feel it to heal it."

Finally, I reached the end of the letter, where I said goodbye. That's when I really felt like I was throwing that heavy burden off me. I said goodbye to my cousin, goodbye to it all.

**Healing Trauma Reminder: Imagining saying goodbye to your perpetrator after telling him or her everything you need to say is a powerful way to release the burden you've been carrying.**

Something else happened in the midst of this whole process. While imagining my cousin sitting in that empty chair and then writing my letter of forgiveness to him, I was actually able to feel a degree of compassion and empathy. All those horrific things he did to me, well, that behavior had to come from somewhere. Things were done to him before anything he did to me. I understood that. No way did that excuse him for what he did, but I could at least see it in another light.

Don't get me wrong. I still don't *like* my cousin, and I definitely don't love the fact that he tried to destroy my whole life for his benefit. I still don't trust him, and I'm definitely not going to be inviting him over for dinner. I haven't spoken with him at the many family weddings and funerals I've attended over the past forty-plus years, and I probably never will. But something in my attitude had begun to shift. I really got that I was an adult and that my abuser was another person who had probably been traumatized. And he couldn't hurt me anymore.

Believe it or not, this was just the beginning of this forgiveness process. After I finished the last step with my cousin, I moved right on to follow the same exercise with my sister. I spent time processing my feelings about those years of sexual and physical abuse I suffered at her hands. I invited her into the empty chair to talk directly to her. I sat down to write Sarah a letter of forgiveness, where I again said what needed to be said but was never spoken when I was a kid:

*"If you tried to touch me again, I would physically hurt you and not worry about what my dad said. I must protect and care for myself. Your hurting, shaming and abusing me wasn't my fault for wanting a sister. Not my fault at all. It's yours for hurting me and taking advantage of me, for abusing and threatening me."*

When I got to the list that began "I forgive you for," I included references like these:

"I forgive you for putting me in the position of choosing between abuse and loneliness."

"I forgive you for ruining the innocence (or what was left of it) of my childhood."

"I forgive you for destroying my trust in women and leading me to take on a love/hate relationship with sex."

When I reached the goodbye section of this forgiveness letter to my sister Sarah, I wrote, "It's hard to say goodbye to you, not so much to you as a person but rather to what I had hoped for that never was."

I was reminded that after everything that she had done to me, she was still my sister. I hated how she hurt me, but, in a way, I still loved her. She was family. The abuse I survived with her was a burden that I carried, but it wasn't as heavy as the burden that had been draped over my shoulders from my cousin.

I wrote letters to a few other people who had hurt me. I also wrote a letter to forgive God because for years I kept wrestling with the desire to blame him for not protecting me.

With each exercise during this major period of counseling, I kept releasing chunks and chunks of pain, sadness, shame, guilt, fear and so much more. Mountains of all that weight of pain and shame seemed to just tumble right off me or dissolve into space. Yeah, I was definitely becoming more and more unbound.

**Scripture:**

**Psalm 23 NIV**

*The Lord is my shepherd, I lack nothing.*

*He makes me lie down in green pastures,*

*He leads me beside quiet waters, He refreshes my soul.*

*He guides me along the right paths*

*for His name's sake.*

*Even though I walk through the darkest valley,*

*I will fear no evil, for You are with me;*

*your rod and your staff, they comfort me.*

*You prepare a table before me in the presence of my enemies.*

*You anoint my head with oil; my cup overflows.*

*Surely Your goodness and love will follow me all the days of my life,*

*and I will dwell in the house of the Lord forever.*

> **Insight for Loved Ones: When we're healing our trauma, our emotions may be spilling out all over the place, or we may neglect our responsibilities. But if you can give us space and grace as we trudge along, everyone will make it to the other side more whole.**

Again, none of these changes happened overnight. This counseling work with Greg wasn't something that was over and done with after a few weeks, or even a few months. No, it actually lasted for two *years*. I stuck with it because of how committed I was to following through with everything this counseling offered me. It was so important to me that I complete this phase of healing that, despite our extremely limited funds, I paid for an entire year of counseling sessions in advance. I was going after that atomic bomb of healing, an explosion to blow decades of trauma symptoms to dust.

I also accepted Greg's suggestion to go on medication to support my healing. He/we discovered during the counseling work that I had anxiety and Attention Deficit Disorder (ADD), which, left untreated, were making my healing work extremely difficult to get through. That was very helpful for me as well. (The use of medication is something that should only be considered through consultation with a qualified healthcare professional.)

I know that this process, and the way I stuck with it for so long, may not be the kind of approach that fits for every guy dealing with some kind of trauma in life. But this is who I am. I like to shoot for something big. I want to squeeze every ounce of healing out of the bottle.

As you follow your healing path, you'll be making your own decisions about the kinds of approaches and beliefs to try on, and at what pace you want to proceed. Maybe you're the kind of guy who wants to keep his eyes out for something big like the empty chair and forgiveness work I went through, or maybe you're someone who needs to go much slower, taking on bits and pieces of healing a little at a time, trying to bring new changes into your life gradually.

> **Healing Trauma Reminder: You get to choose how you pursue your healing and the rhythm and pace that's right for you.**

That's the beauty of being on the healing path. You get to decide where it goes, who to listen to, and how much to take on at any time. Oh, and remember that part I mentioned in the last chapter about the importance of marking your progress along the way? That's something I knew I had to do when I finished the empty chair and forgiveness letters.

**Scripture:**

**James 1:12 MSG**

*Anyone who meets a testing challenge head-on and manages to stick it out is mighty fortunate. For such persons loyally in love with God, the reward is life and more life.*

So, on the day of my last session, December 19, 2011, I decided to have a celebration. Almost like a graduation. I brought in my wife Laura and my sons Jeremiah and Jaden. Everybody got all dressed up.

I knew this was a pivotal day in my recovery and healing, and I wanted to take something tangible away to remind me of where I had been and where I was going. My takeaway was to make a necklace, which I still wear today. This necklace has three symbols:

1) conquering your trauma; 2) stepping into lionhood; 3) finding your voice.

Conquering trauma was simply a way to represent all the work I had done from that day I first decided to check out my first 12-Step meeting through this latest round of healing with the empty chair and forgiveness letters. I never had one simple battle plan. I just kept doing what I believed I had to do to get better, to get my life back.

Stepping into lionhood was my way of saying that from that point on, I was going to be walking into a life of being who I really am. The lion image came out of an experience I had while on a safari in Kenya. While others in our group stuck to the tourist activities, I hung out with one of the Maasai warriors. Later, Willy, our Kenyan guide, told me that I was courageous because I would just plunge in and engage in whatever was in front of me. Courageous like a lion.

**Biblical Insight:**

**God gives us freedom**

God knows when we're victims, and He frees us from the vicious cycle of sin and death imposed upon us by those who've harmed us.

**Scripture:**

**Romans 8: 1, 2 TLB**

*So there is now no condemnation awaiting those who belong to Christ Jesus. For the power of the life-giving Spirit—and this power is mine through Christ Jesus—has freed me from the vicious circle of sin and death.*

**Biblical Insight:**

**Freedom results in blessing.**

What does blessing look like? It's the ability to occupy our own emotions, thoughts, and plans with good works so we can feel true happiness and meet the needs of other hurting people.

**1 Timothy 6: 18, 19 TLB**

*… They should be rich in good works and should give happily to those in need, always being ready to share with others whatever God has given them. By doing this they will be storing up real treasure for themselves in heaven—it is the only safe investment for eternity! And they will be living a fruitful Christian life down here as well.*

Finding your voice was about making a statement about my future work in the world. Now that I was breaking free from more of the shackles, and becoming unbound, just who did I want to be, how did I want to express myself, and what gifts might I be able to offer to others?

Those are the questions I committed to holding. And I've got to tell you, they were much better questions to bounce around my head than all the other stuff that used to fill up my brain. Questions like: How do I get rid of this shame? Why am I still in so much pain?

Yep, I was stepping into a new frontier. My hope for you is that someday you will make the same kind of big, bold step in your life.

**<u>Prayer:</u>**

Father,

Thank You for removing all condemnation in my life. Never again will I carry the burden of guilt, pain, trauma, and abuse that others have inflicted on me. I choose to release them from a debt they can never repay. I ask that You deal with those who've harmed me with Your mercy. Because I choose to respect You and obey Your word, You will continue to restore me in the joy of salvation.

It is the *joy* of the Lord that is my strength! I am conquering my trauma. I have stepped into lionhood and found my voice. I am unbound! Every day, I become more and more free! In Jesus' name,

Amen.

## 12

# BREAKING FREE FROM THE SHACKLES

### BY BECOMING MORE OF WHO WE ARE

*"Our wounds are often the openings into the best and most beautiful parts of ourselves."*

- David Richo, PhD, psychotherapist

When we're living with the pain and suffering caused by trauma, our whole life is usually fixated on one gigantic, constant goal: get rid of the pain!

For a time, we may fall into a pattern of trying to numb the pain with addictions or other unhealthy behavior. Or we try to outrun it by achieving financial success or a high level of prestige. Or we look for some way to shove it to the side, act like the suffering isn't really crippling our lives when it is. Hopefully, we finally reach that point of seeking to recover from and heal all that pain and suffering. When that happens, our one and only goal changes to something new: to heal and get better.

Then, somewhere along the trail that we follow after setting our sights on healing, and I can't tell you when or how, we wake up to a new reality:

*Now I'm free to start reaching for something more. I can imagine new possibilities. I can take steps toward new directions in my life. I can replace what used to be pain with a sense of purpose and meaning. I can start becoming more of who I really am.*

That's an exciting time, whether it comes all at once or little by little. Becoming unbound means being free to become the person we're meant to be, and that's one of the greatest gifts that we give to ourselves. We receive that gift because we have committed to our recovery and healing.

There's just one thing you need to keep in mind about entering into this new place. The answers to the questions about what those new possibilities and directions will be, or what you're supposed to do to live with more meaning and purpose, don't get handed to you in a neat, gold-trimmed certificate. You've still gotta figure it out. And even after you start getting some answers, the new directions you choose to follow may not always go exactly where you hoped. Or they don't take you there as fast as you want. That's just life. But the way I look at it, that sure beats life when you're dragged down into a pit of misery from unresolved trauma!

I'll tell you how this new way of approaching life went for me. After I completed my major round of healing with Greg, I knew I was ready for something totally different. I just didn't know what it was. I did know that I had to figure it out pretty fast because my "graduation day" at the end of that counseling also happened to be the day I had been downsized. I had lost my latest job in a long string of jobs that didn't end well.

So, I just did what I had been doing all along on my healing path: ask for help. Over the years I have built a whole team of helpers into my life: sponsors for my addiction recovery; an ADD coach who helps me navigate around challenges and blessings delivered by my Attention Deficit Disorder; business mentors and coaches; and a whole lot more. At that time in my life, the person who was probably the most important member of my helping team was Rita, my spiritual director.

**Healing Trauma Reminder: Bring helpers into your life, people you can trust and call upon when you've hit a new place you can't *figure* out on your own.**

I had met Rita when I was running that program to improve the lives of Native American youths. Rita was leading a teen drop-in center in Seattle and was a natural and gifted mentor to her staff and others who knew her. You could be real with Rita and she was real with you. She had already helped me at times when I had felt troubled or lost, so when I couldn't find my answer about what to do and where to go after losing my job on the same day that I was "graduating" from the atomic bomb version of healing, I naturally reached out to her again.

"Matt, you've spent the last twenty years of your life recovering from trauma, loss and addiction, and you've helped hundreds of men do the same," Rita said. "You're so easy to talk to, so easy to trust. You share your story so openly. And you care. I believe that you being downsized on the very day you completed your healing work was destiny."

"Go on," I urged. "I'm listening." Admittedly, I was not yet all that impressed.

"It's time to expand this healing work beyond you and the individual men you talk to when they're looking for help," Rita added. "You have the opportunity to build something that can help hundreds or even thousands of men and their families heal from their pain and suffering. You can help other men walk free in their lives, just as you've begun to walk free."

And that's when I accepted this mission to help men heal. The whole idea sank in more and more. If I had survived all kinds of trauma and committed years and years to healing from that trauma, it just made sense that I could find purpose and meaning by leading other men to break free from the shackles of their own trauma.

**Biblical Insight:**

**God has a purpose for us**

It will serve us well to remember that God never wastes one ounce of pain. He will use it all to further His plans and purposes. As we heal, we build the character to lead others out of the bondage of addiction and trauma and into the freedom of being all God created us to be.

**Scripture:**

**Romans 8:28 TLB**

*And we know that all that happens to us is working for our good if we love God and are fitting into his plans.*

**Biblical Insight:**

**A biblical example of leadership**

Leaders are forged in times of difficulty and crisis. The Bible clearly states the character traits God expect of those whom He calls to be the Shepherds of His precious sheep.

**Scripture:**

**Titus 1:7-9 TLB**

*These pastors must be men of blameless lives because they are God's ministers. They must not be proud or impatient; they must not be drunkards or fighters or greedy for money. They must enjoy having guests in their homes and must love all that is good. They must be sensible men, and fair. They must be clean minded and levelheaded. Their belief in the truth that they have been taught must be strong and steadfast so that they will be able to teach it to others and show those who disagree with them where they are wrong.*

> **Insight for Loved Ones: As he continues to become more unbound, don't be surprised if his vocational focus and priorities begin to change.**

Rita's suggestion was backed up by an aptitude test that I took through the Johnson O'Connor Research Foundation. The results told me that being the leader of a cause was a natural fit for me. Yep, this was going to be my new direction.

## The Mission to Help Men Heal

Of course, with my life I always figure that heading in any new direction will probably take me on a whole bunch of unexpected twists and turns. That's definitely what has happened over these last eight years! But I've held firm to the mission and have been doing my best to follow this exciting trail.

The trail guided me through the launch of a nonprofit organization specifically focused on Helping Men Heal, and a related business created to promote awareness and improve services by training clinicians and front-line staff on men healing from trauma. We presented many pioneering educational conferences and seminars, including the "National Male Trauma Healing Leadership Round Table," which brought together educators, treatment providers and policy makers dedicated to increasing awareness and understanding of male trauma.

Our "Victory on the Homefront" event enabled us to honor military veterans who had served our country and come home to heal from trauma, not necessarily combat trauma but traumatic experiences in their personal lives. The same kinds of trauma we've been exploring in this book. These courageous veterans were role models of how to seek out and utilize ways to get better after surviving major trauma, and how to make a positive impact on their families and communities. They were definitely men who were becoming more of who they really were, and their emotional stories brought even hard-core military guys to tears.

In 2016, we helped organize the "Black Men and Boys Healing Summit," an inspirational gathering that shined a spotlight on the devastating effects of unresolved male trauma and urged more civic engagement on behalf of black males. Our message to the attendees was that by helping men heal the invisible wounds of the black community, we were improving outcomes for us all.

Over the last few years, that work has evolved into The Well for Healing Trauma. This project, which I currently serve as Chairman of the Board, is designed to support both men and women in their healing from trauma, and it's steering that effort on university campuses in the form of The Well Healingscape. This therapeutic landscape garden includes a water feature and several stations designed to facilitate healing and education for those who have experienced trauma and loss. The Well is a safe and healing space for students, university staff and faculty, the entire university and the broader metro community.

This Healing Garden that will be located on university campuses focuses on The Five Pillars:

- **Recognizing** trauma and introducing the possibility of accepting it as our trauma.

- **Remembering** and processing memories and trauma by witnessing our story—not just the visible journey known to many but the invisible journey we may have hidden from ourselves.

- **Reconciling** our trauma by beginning to pursue harmony and balance on our journey toward healing.

- **Releasing** unresolved pain, failures, hurts, labels, traumas, losses, and disappointments. Letting go of the burden that trauma has had on us.

- **Reclaiming** ourselves, our loved ones, and our communities.

The first three pillars relate to what we talked about very early in this book with the steps of Awareness, Acceptance and Action that open the door to healing from trauma. The last two pillars, Releasing and Reclaiming, are linked to what we've been covering in the last couple of chapters.

**Gracie's Corner** will be a place to memorialize loss where there is no tangible way to do so. Examples would be women and men who have experienced loss due to a miscarriage, or those who wish to recognize and memorialize missing children.

Because these therapeutic landscape gardens will be built on college campuses, there will be specific healing components related to sexual assault and suicide. Those are major issues for student populations on college and university campuses all over the country.

I'm excited about the possibilities of reaching young people as well as entire metro areas through The Well. Remember, the average length of time it takes for men between suffering trauma and getting help for healing that trauma is twenty-five years. I figure that if we can reach men, and women too, while they're young adults, that gap of time until healing from trauma begins can be chopped to a fraction of that length. And when students start dealing with trauma that young, they'll have so much more opened up to them in their lives. I hope to be speaking at colleges and universities in every state in the country.

## Helping Incarcerated Men to Heal

I'm also grateful for my new opportunities to take the message of the vital importance of men healing from trauma into prisons. Through my speaking engagements in prison communities, I'm following up on my interest in prisoners born from a prison ministry I participated in through East Hill Church back in the 1990s. At that time, we were seeking to guide these men toward a greater understanding of how an obsession with pornography often numbs guys from trauma and pain.

Before I began spending time around prisoners, I just thought men were in there because they had done something wrong. As I discovered, that was only part of the explanation. Most of them were also there because something had been done to them. They had probably just projected their pain onto somebody or something else. I believed that if they could get help in tracing their symptoms to the root cause of the trauma they had survived, they could start on their own healing paths and make positive changes in their lives.

I'm hopeful that this book and my in-person talks at prisons will encourage thousands of men who have been incarcerated to start doing what they need to do to get better. It's exciting to imagine what can happen if more and more men who have spent time behind bars can steer clear of prison after serving their sentence so that they can begin making more meaningful contributions to those they love and the communities they live in.

I intend to remind these men that it doesn't matter what kind of trauma they suffered, or how long ago it happened. It doesn't matter what they remember and what they don't. The only thing that matters is that they decide to get help.

> **Insight for Loved Ones: To gain more compassion for any man in your life who is hurting you, himself and others, try reframing the nagging question in your mind, "What's wrong with him?" to "What happened to him?"**

In my mission to help men heal from trauma and loss, I'm also continuing to help men through one-on-one contact. I'm always willing to provide encouraging words and useful tips to individual men that I happen to meet in my daily life or those who seek me out individually. That's just who I am and what I do. So many people have stopped to offer help and guidance to me in my healing, this is just one way that I can give back.

> **Healing Trauma Reminder: If other people have helped you on your healing journey, you may want to consider ways for you to give back.**

I've got a bunch of other plans, ideas and hopes for other new ventures that could become part of my mission. I expect to follow this book with one, two, maybe several related books on specific subjects with the theme of helping men heal. Beyond that, I envision a TV show, a comprehensive website of resources for men and a whole lot more. Stay tuned!

This rundown of my new professional endeavors paints at least part of the picture of what I've been up to since I began steering my life toward becoming more of who I am. I've also had some losses, failures and setbacks since I took on this mission to help men heal. I wouldn't be surprised if I have more of them. But there's no way that any setback will make me abandon my mission.

## Biblical Insight:

### A biblical example of what a healed man looks like

A healed man is humble, comforted, just, and good. He is also kind, merciful, and pure of heart, and he strives for peace defined as wholeness in every area of life. A healed man can't help but produce good deeds.

## Scripture:

### Matthew 5:1-16 TLB

*One day as the crowds were gathering, He went up the hillside with His disciples and sat down and taught them there.*

*"Humble men are very fortunate!" He told them, "for the Kingdom of Heaven is given to them. Those who mourn are fortunate! for they shall be comforted. The meek and lowly are fortunate! for the whole wide world belongs to them.*

*"Happy are those who long to be just and good, for they shall be completely satisfied. Happy are the kind and merciful, for they shall be shown mercy. Happy are those whose hearts are pure, for they shall see God. Happy are those who strive for peace—they shall be called the sons of God. Happy are those who are persecuted because they are good, for the Kingdom of Heaven is theirs.*

*"When you are reviled and persecuted and lied about because you are my followers—wonderful! Be happy about it! Be very glad! for a tremendous reward awaits you up in heaven. And remember, the ancient prophets were persecuted too.*

*"You are the world's seasoning, to make it tolerable. If you lose your flavor, what will happen to the world? And you yourselves will be thrown out and trampled underfoot as worthless. You are the world's light—a city on a hill, glowing in the night for all to see. Don't hide your light! Let it shine for all; let your good deeds glow for all to see, so that they will praise your heavenly Father."*

## Free to Dream Again

How about you? What changes are you noticing in your life that are reminding you that your healing has progressed and you are becoming more of who you are? It doesn't matter if those changes are personal, professional or anything else. It doesn't matter if you can pinpoint some big-time mission you're going to take on, or you're just noticing how things in your life are different. Better somehow.

Maybe you're building healthier relationships. Maybe you're making new friends or expanding your circle of supporters and contacts. Maybe you wake up in the morning and actually feel ready to imagine good things in your life instead of another day of pain and misery. Just allowing yourself to dream of something new is part of becoming more of who you are because when we suffer trauma, it often feels like that ability to dream has been taken away from us forever.

You also might be finding that you have suddenly developed new character traits or abilities that you never had before. When we're doing the work to become more unbound, we tend to develop greater perseverance to keep chugging along the path through all the challenges. We come away with more gratitude for the people and tools that helped get us through. Or we discover the power of forgiveness to get the weight of anger or resentment toward people in our lives off our backs. Taking aptitude testing can help you access your own awareness of yourself and help set you on a clearer path.

If you're the kind of guy who turned to wacky humor as one way to deal with the struggles of trying to heal, you may come away with more playfulness. Or passion. Or patience. Or just the desire to reach out and help others dealing with the same kind of stuff you had to deal with, because you know that you've become part of something that's bigger than you.

**Scripture:**

**1 Corinthians 2:9 CEV**

*What God has planned for people who love Him is more than eyes have seen or ears have heard. It has never even entered our minds!*

> **Healing Trauma Reminder: Take inventory of the new strengths and new ways of looking at life that show up when you become more unbound, and allow yourself to imagine where they might lead you.**

Some professionals describe the process of healing from trauma as getting turned right-side up after we've been knocked down. I'm not sure it's that simple. The thing is, even if our life feels somehow like it's been turned right-side up, it's not the same life. It's not like fixing a flat tire and getting our car back up and running in the same way it used to before the blowout. We're changed, for sure, but we still have a scar from surviving our trauma. Maybe that scar itches sometimes, and perhaps other people can still see it on us. Hopefully, we can look at that scar as only a symbol of where we have been, something that we can accept as we head in the new directions that we are free to follow.

## Bringing Healing Back Home

For me, those new directions go beyond my mission to help men heal. They also extend into my personal life.

As an example, I've been continuing to heal the racial divide inside of me. Being born half-white and half-black, I used to feel like I didn't really belong in either world. Now, my perspective is totally different. I'll give you one simple example. Before our family's recent move to Seattle, I had been attending two different churches around Vancouver, Washington. One was an all-white (except for me) Presbyterian Church, the other an all-black charismatic church. I felt at home in both churches and the different groups of people who attended them because I have really embraced being half-white and half-black. I understand and relate to both worlds much better in many of my personal and professional endeavors.

Another way that I keep striving to be bigger in my personal life is to be the best husband and father I can be. As my pastor Ted once told me, when I arrive at the gates of heaven God isn't going to ask me about my financial or vocational achievements. He's going to ask, "Did you help make your wife and her life more beautiful than when I brought her to you?" I continue to let those words guide me, and I've really appreciated all the ways that Laura has been a big helper on many of my important ventures.

I embrace a responsibility to help all those I love claim greater health and well-being in their own lives. With my two sons, I try to tell them as often as I can that I love them, that I'm proud of them, that I'm glad they are my sons. That's a message I would have welcomed hearing every day from my own dad. When we are healing from trauma and becoming more of who we are, it's natural to give those we love everything we wish had been given to us.

While our kids were growing up, we were a real Disney family, spending many Christmases at Disneyland and even buying a time share there. Why? Well, Disney is a lot of fun for kids, but it was also important for me because I never got to Disneyland when I was growing up.

With my boys, as I mentioned earlier, I encourage them to become aware of what they are feeling and not be afraid of expressing those emotions. My sons cry, and I reassure them that it's totally oaky for boys to do so.

I've also been blessed with a change in how I relate to my own dad. After I began to get more comfortable with what I was doing and who I was becoming on my healing path, I challenged him:

"How come all these people in my recovery groups, people who were perfect strangers until I started going there, can hug me and tell me that they love me, but you can't?" I asked. Today, every time we're on the phone together, my dad makes it a point to tell me that he loves me. When we're together physically, he always gives me a hug goodbye just before I leave. And he and my mom have been extremely generous in assisting me when my career twists and turns have left our family in need.

How does this relate to your own healing path? Are you more capable of telling loved ones that you love them? Are you making an effort to surround yourself with people who care about you and aren't afraid to tell you that?

When we're not caught up in our own private pain and suffering, we just appreciate family more. It's like we've got more space inside of us to feel those important connections. That's another great benefit of breaking free from the shackles of trauma and becoming more unbound.

## "My Sister Died!"

My sister Sarah, the sister who had abused me for years, died in 2003. Actually, she was murdered. When I heard the news, I have to admit that any sadness that I may have felt was mixed with a strong sense of relief. After all, she had been a perpetrator when I was a vulnerable child. After she was taken from our family, I had very little contact with her. When I saw her once early in high school, I still felt pain, fear and anger. When she tracked me down once while I was attending college, I hardly even spoke to her. I mean, what do you say to a person who caused you so much trauma and grief, right?

But after I completed that empty chair exercise and wrote my letter of forgiveness to Sarah, my perspective changed. First, I got curious enough to look up articles about what happened to her. Without going into all the details, I learned that she had continued to live a very hard life as an adult. Her murder apparently came out of some kind of drug deal. I thought about all that.

Then, one day while riding to my office, a sudden feeling poured over me.

"My sister died!" I said to myself. "My *sister* died!"

Instead of anger or bitterness toward my sister, I now felt grief. Sudden, intense grief. In that one moment, and over the following days and weeks, it was like Sarah had reclaimed her identity in my life as my sister. She wasn't just my perpetrator any more, she was that young girl who had walked into our house carrying nothing but one little suitcase and a Raggedy Ann doll. We were still connected; she was family.

Before long, I found myself in a grief support group to deal with this deep sense of loss. I also began to spend hours researching my sister's past. When I learned that she had four children, I decided I needed to find them, introduce myself, maybe even see how I could help them. I've met all of Sarah's kids and am working, however imperfectly and slowly, on developing an ongoing relationship with them.

That process is still unfolding, and I don't honestly know where it will lead. But I do know that before I committed to my healing path, even the possibility of this kind of connection was unthinkable. That's the way it happens when you become unbound and you get bigger . . . and bigger.

**Scripture:**

**Psalm 34:18, 19 MEV**

*The Lord is near to the broken-hearted, and saves the contrite of spirit. Many are the afflictions of the righteous, but the Lord delivers him out of them all.*

## Life Just Becomes More Alive

So, life just keeps expanding, and you keep on becoming more of who you are, and nothing bad is ever going to happen to you again, right? Ha! We know life doesn't work that way. New challenges will come along; no one is ever immune from pain and struggle.

I got hit with that reminder big-time when I was diagnosed with colorectal cancer. As I shared with you in the chapter about medical trauma, I've had to ride through all the physical and emotional struggles everyone faces on the cancer roller-coaster. But even when I'm getting tossed around by this latest trauma, I have seen how my whole life perspective is different from before. And my care and appreciation for the doctors, nurses and specialists that led me through the cancer healing process can't be understated!

Signs of positive change show up in my life in many different ways. First, I'm better able to process my emotions. And on this ride, I've had a boatload of them. Whenever I first start walking in the hospital again after some treatment or surgery, I find myself just naturally paying attention to what I am feeling and allowing myself to feel it while I walk. Does that mean I'm turning cartwheels in the corridor and shouting, "This is crazy, I'm having my feelings!" Uh, not exactly. But I do feel more aware and more whole somehow. I'm more in touch with this experience of living with cancer, and that makes me feel bigger somehow too.

I'm also better able to pay attention to what I need to do to stay as healthy as possible, not just physically healthy but emotionally healthy too. When my bad eating habits spiked while dealing with my cancer, I went right to Overeaters Anonymous. When I found myself working 80-hour weeks again in the middle of my cancer treatments, I got in touch with my Workaholics Anonymous sponsor.

And when my wife Laura gently asked me, "Does it bother you that you have cancer in the same place in your body where you were abused?", I didn't run from the question. I thought about it and, well, yes, it *did* bother me. I got in touch with a counselor to process that.

I've also tried to deal with how it feels to look up survival rates for my type of cancer and come away feeling like I should be telling people, "If you call me five years from now, there's a seventy percent chance I'll answer the phone." Anything is possible, but if that's the way it plays out, I have goals of what I would like to do with my wife and children before it's too late. Personal goals.

Becoming more of who you are, or who God intended you to be, does not make life perfect. It makes life fuller. More whole. More

. . alive.

**Prayer:**

Father,

Every day You wipe away another tear and take away more of the pain. Every day I become more and more like the image of Your son, Jesus. Every day, I become freer.

I am constantly being strengthened by the power of Your might! You live big in me! I can overcome all things! I am a blessing to You, to my family, and to my sphere of influence. In Jesus' name,

Amen.

## 13

## WHEN MEN HEAL FROM TRAUMA, EVERYBODY WINS

*"Once you choose hope, anything is possible."*

- Christopher Reeve

We're coming toward the end of our time together. I hope that reading this book has helped you find your own way to understand trauma and discover the many paths to follow in healing from your pain and suffering.

I'm confident that you can now see how acknowledging and addressing trauma and loss that you have survived isn't a process that's "out there" or far away. Healing from trauma is not something that's available only to a certain few guys, the ones who are really smart or super-rich or just built in such a way that they can deal with this kind of stuff. The opportunity and the resources to heal from trauma are available right here, right now, totally accessible to every guy. That might have sounded impossible to you in the past, but now you know that healing really is possible . . . for *you*.

It doesn't matter how old you are. It doesn't matter how much money you have. It doesn't matter how many years it's been since you suffered trauma. It doesn't matter how many mistakes you've made when you were doing your best to survive while carrying the invisible wounds of trauma. It doesn't matter if you've gotten yourself in trouble and wound up in prison, or you've spent years imprisoned in pain and hopelessness.

You now have the awareness, the ideas and the reminders that I have been sharing to help you start down the path to healing, and to keep on following it. Your road to recovery and healing won't look like mine—at least I hope it isn't filled with as many twists and turns as the journey that I have been following all these years. You'll find your own way on that healing path, the journey that will lead to greater peace, self-acceptance, freedom from shame. And so much more.

You know something, a lot actually, about breaking free from the shackles and becoming unbound. You've uncovered a message that every guy who has been knocked down by trauma is free to discover:

> **To live without our heaviest burdens, to be unshackled, to be free, is the greatest gift in the world. No money can buy this gift. You only have to want it, do the work and be willing to receive it.**

One of the most rewarding things about this gift is that it doesn't end with us as individuals. Breaking free from the shackles of trauma helps generations of people close to us to be free.

I still believe that one of my biggest achievements in my life is doing a pretty good job so far in not allowing the generational chaos and garbage that had been a part of my life get passed on to my kids. I sure haven't been perfect about that, but my hope is that they have been exposed to only a small percentage of what I experienced, and what they probably would have gotten from me if I had not been committed to healing from my past.

It takes a lot of courage for us as men to even try to stop generational cycles of pain and unhealthy influences. For many of us, it seems like we've felt the pressure of three, four, five generations or more in our families that have struggled with the same addiction, or the same destructive beliefs or behavior. To stake a stand and say, "This stuff stops with me" is a major gift to our family. And to our kids' families. And beyond.

We can be the shining example that says, "We as men do not have to pass on to our kids what got dumped on us. Our past does not have to repeat itself in the future."

**Biblical Insight:**

**Jesus broke all curses over us**

Just as Jesus died on the cross in our place for our sins, He also died on the cross to remove all curses. It does not matter whether a curse has been passed down to us from others or was caused by our own actions. We are redeemed from all curses through Jesus' sacrifice! The generational curse is broken off of us and need not pass on to our future generations. In fact, God's blessing is now passed on down to future generations!

**Scripture:**

**Galatians 3:13, 14 MSG**

*Christ redeemed us from that self-defeating, cursed life by absorbing it completely into himself. Do you remember the Scripture that says, "Cursed is everyone who hangs on a tree"? That is what happened when Jesus was nailed to the cross: He became a curse, and at the same time dissolved the curse. And now, because of that, the air is cleared and we can see that Abraham's blessing is present and available for non-Jews, too. We are all able to receive God's life, his Spirit, in and with us by believing—just the way Abraham received it.*

## The Price of Silence

Every day, I am reminded of the cost that comes when men are not able to summon the strength, the courage and the support to take the steps we have been talking about and seek help and healing from trauma. The pain and suffering caused by unresolved trauma usually goes way beyond that one individual male's life. My friend Peter recently shared with me a tragic story that reminded me of how true this is.

Peter was the oldest male in a family of seven kids growing up in Ohio. With hard work, dedication and a good sense of timing, Peter became a successful business leader. His youngest brother, however, seemed to face constant struggles in life: trouble in school, learning challenges, messed up relationships, inability to maintain a successful career, alcohol and drug addiction and abuse. Peter and his siblings offered their support and encouragement where they could, but, unfortunately, their efforts were not enough. For years, Peter wondered what had gone wrong in Scott's life. It just seemed to have gone off the rails.

Finally, decades along into adulthood, an answer emerged. Peter got a call from one his sisters who asked to visit him as soon as possible. "Scott was sexually abused," she said. She explained that it had all started when he was eight years old and that it had gone on for ten years. The abuser was John, his brother-in-law. Scott had never told anyone for thirty years . . . until now.

As Peter soon learned, Scott had kept his abuse secret all that time because he had been afraid that if Peter's father had found out, he would have killed John. And now, John was caring for his six-year-old grandson every day after school, grooming this young boy just as he had groomed Scott. Knowing that this grandson was in danger of being abused as Scott had been, Peter, his wife, his sister and her husband resolved to bring the situation into the light. They immediately began to tell the rest of the family what had happened to Scott, in the hopes of stopping the cycle of abuse.

Telling the truth about the history of Scott's abuse sparked a firestorm that went on for a number of years, fracturing family relationships. The secret was initially kept from Peter's mother, but she felt something had gone terribly wrong in the family and kept asking, "Are you not telling me something?" Finally, it was agreed to break the news to her. While it hurt her terribly, she finally understood why Scott was so different and had struggled so much more than her other children.

Peter's family was tormented with questions: Why did this happen? Why didn't Scott come forward and tell us when it was happening? How would his life have turned out better if the truth had come out when he was still young and he had found the help he needed? Most of those questions were never resolved.

The truth, however, did ultimately pave the way for positive changes. Once the secret was out, Scott began to heal from his trauma. He attended AA and stopped using drugs and alcohol; and he found deep faith in Jesus. He asked the family to forgive John, just as he had reconciled with John about six years after his secret became public. Sadly, Scott was diagnosed with a terrible, incurable fatal illness, but he passed away at peace with God his maker, and with John, the trusted family member who had so damaged his life.

Peter's family deeply mourned their loss, but that firestorm and the full price of silence was felt for years. Peter's family eventually forgave John, although they could not forget what he had done to Scott and didn't accept him back into the family. Gradually, however, those old wounds began to heal. Peter says the most important part of what happened after the news about the abuse finally came to the surface is that the cycle finally was stopped.

I met Peter through church, and when he learned of my mission to help men heal, he offered to assist me in any way he could. In his day-to-day life, he kept his eyes wide open for young people like Scott who showed signs of suffering trauma. It was too late to help his own brother, but maybe Peter could take what he had learned from his family's tragedy and use it to help somebody else.

Then, through his work on a truancy board in his community, Peter saw an opportunity. A boy who had once been an excellent student until two years earlier had stopped going to school. He closed himself up in his bedroom playing video games and watching TV all day and night, coming out only for one meal a day.

"Did something happen two years ago?" Peter asked this boy's mom. Boom! The truth stormed out of the gate where it had been locked inside. This boy who had gone from loving school to hiding from life had been sexually abused. Help and support arrived from many circles. The boy was transferred to a new school and was soon excelling again. As he explained to Peter, he had found a teacher who loved him.

Love, caring, awareness, understanding, a willingness to take action on behalf of the child that had survived trauma. It had all come together. A young boy's life had been turned around, and his family, his classmates, his teachers, his entire community all benefitted. As that young boy grows into adulthood, he will have opportunities that, sadly, Peter's brother did not have for so many years.

Listening to Peter's story, I thought about the steep price paid by men, and their loved ones, when they remain silent. When they stay tight-lipped about trauma they have suffered. When they don't reach out for help and start on the healing path.

**Insight for Loved Ones: Bringing to light ugly and painful family secrets, in the right way, can bring healing to the entire family and help prevent what happened from being passed down to the next generations.**

Sometimes, men or boys pay the ultimate price: taking their own life. Nobody has to tell guys like Gary about that ultimate price of silence. As we discovered earlier in this book, Gary lost his college-age son to suicide.

Those stories of the price men pay for silence always sadden all who are directly impacted by them, and all who hear about them. I hear many of these stories in the work that I do, and they remind me of the urgency of guiding more men whose lives have been damaged by trauma to the door that opens up to a world of healing and wholeness. A more peaceful and more fulfilling life. A life with more satisfaction and joy.

I am also fortunate enough to hear many stories that bring to life the amazing changes in the lives of men who do step onto the healing path. And keep following it wherever they need to go. These stories give me hope, keep me going in this mission to encourage and support men who have survived trauma to get the help they need. Today!

**Biblical Insight:**

**A biblical example of how Joseph's decision made everyone a winner**

Joseph is the perfect example of an "everybody wins" situation. He was restored to his father, and the brothers who did him harm were the very ones that Joseph saved. In fact, he saved his entire clan AND the entire nation of Egypt! He preserved the line from which the Messiah would come!

**Story:**

**Genesis 50: 14-26 MSG**

*After burying his father, Joseph went back to Egypt. All his brothers who had come with him to bury his father returned with him. After the funeral, Joseph's brothers talked among themselves: "What if Joseph is carrying a grudge and decides to pay us back for all the wrong we did him?"*

*So they sent Joseph a message, "Before his death, your father gave this command: Tell Joseph, 'Forgive your brothers' sin—all that wrongdoing. They did treat you very badly.' Will you do it? Will you forgive the sins of the servants of your father's God?"*

*When Joseph received their message, he wept.*

*Then the brothers went in person to him, threw themselves on the ground before him and said, "We'll be your slaves."*

*Joseph replied, "Don't be afraid. Do I act for God? Don't you see, you planned evil against me but God used those same plans for my good, as you see all around you right now—life for many people. Easy now, you have nothing to fear; I'll take care of you and your children." He reassured them, speaking with them heart-to-heart.*

*Joseph continued to live in Egypt with his father's family. Joseph lived 110 years. He lived to see Ephraim's sons into the third generation. The sons of Makir, Manasseh's son, were also recognized as Joseph's.*

*At the end, Joseph said to his brothers, "I am ready to die. God will most certainly pay you a visit and take you out of this land and back to the land he so solemnly promised to Abraham, Isaac, and Jacob."*

*Then Joseph made the sons of Israel promise under oath, "When God makes his visitation, make sure you take my bones with you as you leave here."*

*Joseph died at the age of 110 years. They embalmed him and placed him in a coffin in Egypt.*

## Sharing the Gift of Healing

Healing from trauma really is a gift that we give to ourselves. And a gift that sends out ripples in wider and wider circles all around us.

For those of us who are adults, that gift definitely extends out to our loved ones. In my work in helping men heal, I find over and over that no one is more excited and supportive about men becoming healthier and more whole than the loved ones who care about them. Loved ones just naturally appreciate and enjoy seeing the men they know becoming more present, more engaged in their relationships, more confident, more at peace with themselves and the world around them. And because we as men have been the primary ones projecting our trauma onto them, our healing helps to create a safe space for them to more deeply engage their own healing journey.

So, your gift of healing from trauma and becoming unbound is not just an individual thing. Those little ripples of health, wholeness and hope reach those we know and even those we don't know. And when more and more guys like us do that, we can start becoming part of a sea change.

I can envision the day when men everywhere go from resisting trauma recovery to embracing trauma recovery. I know it's possible. I've lived it. I've witnessed it with other men, again and again.

When that change comes, it will mean less poverty. Less crimes of violence. Less suicide.

I envision a world where trauma, loss, neglect and deep hurt experienced by men will be recognized, acknowledged and addressed. A world where our partners, our kids, our parents, our friends and our communities are all becoming healthier, stronger, safer.

Because we as men are choosing to be vulnerable. Because we as men are choosing to seek help. Because we as men are choosing to heal.

That's the choice that stands in front of you today. Right now. You can launch or continue to march along on a journey that will lead you to the place where you too may proclaim that making the choice to address the major trauma and loss in your life and follow the healing path is the greatest accomplishment in your life.

You hold the key that unlocks that door to healing and wholeness, to peace and joy, to the ripples of positive change that enrich the lives of everybody around you. I have faith that you're going to use that key. And join this mission. And extend the healing and wholeness that pours into your life out to a wider and wider circle of men.

And when that happens, I want to hear all about it!

**Scripture:**

**Jeremiah 29:11-14 NLT**

*For I know the plans I have for you, says the Lord. They are plans for good and not for disaster, to give you a future and a hope. In those days when you pray, I will listen. If you look for me wholeheartedly, you will find me. I will be found by you, says the Lord. I will end your captivity and restore your fortunes...*

**Prayer:**

Father,

I can do all things through Christ who strengthens me. Thank You for keeping me in Your power. Thank You for the good plans that You have in store for me.

Thank You for listening to my cries and coming to my rescue. Thank You for answering my prayers and giving me victory over every trauma. In Jesus' name,

Amen.

# TOOLS THAT HELPED ME

OTE: These are tools and resources that have been useful for me on my healing journey, and I share them here in hopes that you may find some of them helpful for you on your own healing path.

To learn more about any of the references on this list, you may choose to Google them or visit our website:

**TheUnboundMan.com**

Our platform dedicated to being "A Hub and Clearinghouse for Men's Healing".

- **The Five Love Languages** – Learning this has transformed my relationships with my wife and my kids by understanding specifically how they give and receive love.

- **ACE Test (Adverse Childhood Experiences)** – This helps to measure 10 types of childhood trauma and provides increased awareness of the level of trauma we have experienced as a child and how that trauma can affect our future health.

- **Aptitude Testing** – Aptitudes are natural talents, special abilities for doing or learning to do certain kinds of things. The Johnson O'Connor Research Foundation is one resource that offers this kind of testing.

- **Enneagram** – This test is a powerful tool for personal and collective transformation. It shows nine distinct strategies for relating to the self, others and the world. It helped take me from compulsion to contemplation.

- **21 Common Reactions to Trauma** – This was an article that helped me to understand that my reactions to trauma were understandable and normal, based on what I had experienced.

- **12-Step groups** – These are the many addiction recovery programs that all end in "anonymous." There are 12-Step anonymous groups for almost every kind of addiction and hurt.

- **Celebrate Recovery** – This is the Christian Church's version of 12-step recovery.

- **Coachability Self Test** – This is the test I took to help me understand my level of being teachable, as increasing my teachability enhanced my ability to heal.

- **The Feeling Wheel** – The sixty-four feelings, six root feelings tool that I used to help me identify me feelings. This was transformational for me and my sons.

- **Attachment Style** – How we attach or do not attach to others can impact all our relationships. It can include adult relationships, such as friendships, emotional affairs, and adult romantic or platonic relationships, especially with the ones closest to us. Attachment styles helped identify the attachment styles of my wife and me, as well as detailing how our attachment styles were damaging our relationship and specific ways to relate in healing.

- **The Cognitive Triangle** – This tool helped me understand how my thinking patterns, my beliefs and attitudes, my physical sensations, my thoughts and feelings, and my behavior were all interlinked, and in what order to address them.

- **The Couples' Dialogue Tool** – This saved our marriage by giving my wife and me a safe structure to have conflict in a way that mirrored, validated and empathized the other person. We had a copy of The Feeling Wheel when we did this so we could more easily identify what we were feeling.

- **Healing the Inner Child** – There are many tools for this, typically led by a counselor. This work helped me learn to honor and care for the little boy whose identity and self-esteem were shattered by trauma.

- **Using Temptation as an Opportunity for Healing Process** – This helped me to retrain my brain when an addictive temptation would engulf me. It's a tool many Christian counselors use.

- **The Five Stages of Grief** – The stages are Denial, Anger, Bargaining, Depression and Acceptance. There are lots of tools and literature about this. I did this work alone, with a counselor, and in a six-month grief recovery group.

- **The Fight, Flight, Freeze or Appease Response** – The work I did around looking at and understanding my responses to these and other triggers was a game-changer for me.

- **In Conflict I Have Two Choices** – (I learned this in counseling, so it's nothing to Google.) The two choices are: Be a Healing Agent (choose to respond in a way that will help the other person heal); or be a Re-wounding Agent (choose to respond in a way that re-wounds the other person).

- **StrengthsFinder Testing** – Taking this test revealed my five greatest strengths. This has helped me focus on what I am, rather than what I'm not.

- **The Seven Habits of Highly Emotionally Healthy People** article from *Psychology Today* helped me improve my emotional resilience.

- **The Rest Cycle** – This tool and others in Jeff VanVonderen's book *Tired of Trying to Measure Up* have done the most to help me continue to shed shame on a daily basis.

- ***Delivered from Distraction* by Edward Hallowell and John J. Ratey** helped me see the positive attributes of my ADD and maximize them while managing the struggles caused by ADD. I actually ordered their first book, *Driven to Distraction*, the landmark book around ADD, but I got *Delivered from Distraction* in the mail instead.

- At that time in my life, I guess God wanted me to hear more about the solution than the problem.

- **The Speed of Trust by Stephen M.R. Covey** – Reading this book, more than anything else, gave me an objective framework to learn who and how to trust.

- **The Gentle Path through the 12 Steps** – This workbook by Patrick Carnes, along with program-specific literature and a sponsor, is what I've used to work through all three of my addictions.

- **Codependent No More by Melody Beattie** – Helped me find healthier ways to be in relationship with others.

- **Build Your Own Success & Healing Team** – Mine consisted of Life Coach, ADD Coach, Business Leadership Coach, Nonprofit/Cause Focus Mentor, Spiritual Director, Financial Coach/Advisor, Primary Care Doctor, Specific Medical Condition Doctors, Personal Trainer, Massage Therapist, Marriage Coach/Counselor, a Key Teacher involved in each of my kids' lives, Mental Health Counselor. They weren't all used at the same time, but many of them were. Most cost nothing beyond my/their investment of time; others do cost and I utilize them as I'm able to afford them. Life is a team sport.

# SOURCES FOR STATISTICS

Here are sources used for the statistics listed in Chapter 1.

- 61 percent of males have experienced at least one traumatic event in their lives (Ronald C. Kessler, 1995).

- 10 percent of males have experienced *four or more* types of trauma (Ronald C. Kessler, 1995).

- 30 percent of men were physically abused as boys (Adverse Childhood Experience Study, 1998).

- 1 in 6 males have experienced sexual abuse (Adverse Childhood Experience Study, 1998).

- 41 percent of domestic violence victims are men (Centers for Disease Control, 2010).

- 79 percent of suicide victims are males (SAVE – Suicide Awareness Voices of Education).

# BIBLIOGRAPHY/SUGGESTED READING

Barton, Ruth Haley. *Invitation to Solitude and Silence.* Downers Grove, IL: InterVarsity Press, 2004.

Beattie, Melody. *Codependent No More.* Center City, MN: Hazelden, 1986.

Boyd, Randy. *Healing the Man Within.* La Quinta, CA: Courageous Healers Publishing, 2015.

Black, Claudia. *It Will Never Happen to Me.* Center City, MN: Hazelden, 1981.

Cori, Jasmin Lee, MS, CPC. *Healing from Trauma.* Cambridge, MA: Marlowe & Company, 2007.

Covey, Stephen M.R. *The Speed of Trust.* New York: Free Press, 2006.

Covington, Stephanie; Griffin, Dan; and Dauer, Rick. *A Man's Workbook: Helping Men Recover.* San Francisco, CA: Jossey-Bass, 2011.

Coyle, C.T. *Men and Abortion.* Life Cycle Books, Ltd, 1999.

Farrar, Digene. *Not My Secret to Keep: A Memoir of Healing from Childhood Sexual Abuse.* Seattle, WA: Sunsielle Press, 2014.

Figgers, Michael S. *Healing the Hearts of Broken Men*. Denver, CO: Outskirts Press, Inc., 2013.

Fradkin, Howard. *Joining Forces*. Carlsbad, CA: Hay House, Inc., 2012.

Graber, Ken. *Ghosts in the Bedroom*. Deerfield Beach, FL: Health Communications, Inc., 1991.

Hallowell, Edward; and Ratey, John J. *Delivered from Distraction*. New York: Anchor Books, 2011.

Harris, Russ. *The Happiness Trap: How to Stop Struggling and Start Living*. Toronto, ON, Canada. Trumpeter, 2008.

Herman, Judith. *Trauma and Recovery*. Philadelphia, PA: Basic Books, 1992.

Hunter, Mic. *Abused Boys*. Lexington, MA: Lexington Books, 1990.

Kushner, Harold S. *When Bad Things Happen to Good People*. New York: Shocken Books, Inc., 1981.

Lew, Mike. *Victims No Longer*. New York: HarperCollins Publishers Inc., 2004.

Lucado, Max. *You'll Get Through This*. Nashville, TN: Thomas Nelson, 2013.

Lyme. Alan; Powell, David J.; and Andrew, Stephen. *Men's Healing*. West Palm Beach, FL: Hanley Hope, 2008.

Maltz, Wendy. *The Sexual Healing Journey*. New York: Harper Collins Publishers Inc., 1991.

Moore, Wes. *The Other Wes Moore*. New York: Singleton & Grau, 2010.

Seligman, Martin E.P., PhD. *Authentic Happiness*. New York: Atria Paperback, 2002.

VanVonderen, Jeff. *Tired of Trying to Measure Up*. Minneapolis, MN: Bethany House Publishers, 1989.

Worthington, Everett L Jr. *Forgiving and Reconciling*. Downers Grove, IL: InterVarsity Press, 2003.

**Movie:**

*The Mask You Live In,* Director – Jessica Siebel Newsom; Producers

– Jennifer Siebel Newsom, Jessica Cogdon and Jessica Anthony. Release date: Jan. 25, 2015.

## ABOUT THE AUTHOR

Matt Burton's life has been one spent in two different worlds.

A baby born to a white-collar Caucasian mom and a blue-collar African American dad. A childhood that began in the inner city and ended in rural America.

A star basketball player, DJ for Z100 radio, Concordia University graduate, and CEO/founder of several companies, including two created to help men heal from trauma and train clinicians on male trauma and loss.

A trauma survivor, Matt has relentlessly pursued his own healing while helping other men heal. From group homes to college campuses, prisons to board rooms, Matt has helped thousands of men heal and reclaim their lives.

www.ingramcontent.com/pod-product-compliance
Lightning Source LLC
LaVergne TN
LVHW011947060526
838201LV00061B/4238